Holistic Care for Birds

Holistic Care
for Birds

A Manual of Wellness
and Healing

HOWELL BOOK HOUSE

HOWELL BOOK HOUSE

IDG Books Worldwide, Inc.
1633 Broadway
New York, NY 10019

Library of Congress Cataloging-in-Publication Data available upon request.

ISBN: 0-87605-566-8

Manufactured in the United States of America

10 9 8 7 6 5 4 3 2 1

Illustrations by Richard Fox
Production Team: Stephanie Lucas, Marie Kristine Parial-Leonardo, Natalie Evans

For general information on IDG Books Worldwide's books in the U.S., please call our Consumer Customer Service department at 1-800-762-2974. For reseller information, including discounts, bulk sales, customized editions, and premium sales, please call our Reseller Customer Service department at 1-800-434-3422.

DISCLAIMER

This book is not intended as a substitute for the medical advice of veterinarians. The reader should regularly consult an avian veterinarian in matters relating to his or her bird's health, particularly in respect to any symptoms that may require diagnosis or medical attention.

TABLE OF CONTENTS

PREFACE

Those of us who love birds want only the best for them. Because we know that well-educated caregivers are the key to keeping a bird healthy, we wrote this book to explain how you can care for your bird using holistic methods. What you learn can also help you support the holistic avian veterinarian you have chosen to care for your bird's serious ailments. There is no magic in medicine; a loving caregiver provides many of the most important aspects necessary to restore an animal to health. More importantly, an educated, dedicated caregiver can help ensure the continued good health of a beloved companion, his or her bird.

During the last decade we have begun to realize that to offer a bird the finest care it is important to view the bird, whether sick or well, as a whole, taking into account its physical and emotional requirements. This is the basis of holistic care: first acknowledging that each bird is an individual with physical and emotional needs and then agreeing that, by bringing the bird into our lives, we are obligated to meet these needs to the best of our ability. The result benefits both bird and human: the bird is more likely to be happy and healthy in its new home, and the owner can take greater pleasure in the bird.

Holistic care is not new, but it is widely misunderstood. It comprises more than alternative methods such as acupuncture, homeopathy and herbal remedies, although these are part of the whole. A truly holistic approach combines the knowledge and practices of conventional Western medicine with alternative methods that have been used for many centuries worldwide. The fundamental belief in holistic medicine is that the body has the ability to heal itself. The doctor simply aids in the healing process in the least invasive manner possible. The doctor wants to find both the cause of the disease and a way to help the body rid itself of the condition instead of merely eliminating the symptoms.

In general, pet birds can expect to live only about five years. That statistic becomes truly shocking when you realize that some large parrots, such as Cockatoos and Macaws, can live as long as 50 to 75 years or more in the wild. Even small birds, such as Canaries, which can live as long as 15 years in their natural habitat, can expect to survive only a few years in captivity. There are many reasons for this, both emotional and physical, encompassing a lack of research and a poor understanding of several subjects essential to supporting a healthy life, including nutrition, medical, emotional and environmental needs.

We cannot pretend that we know everything about holistic care for pet birds; we learn new ways to help birds every day. We hope to give you an opportunity to improve your bird's quality of life and life expectancy with alternative treatments. Research has shown that living with a pet can extend human life; we must now learn to return the favor.

–*David McCluggage and Pamela Leis Higdon*

ACKNOWLEDGMENTS

The authors would like to thank their respective spouses, Linda and Sherman, for their contributions and support. They are especially indebted to Jennifer Liberts and Nikki Moustaki, who worked patiently with them on this concept for many months, and to Richard Fox for his lovely illustrations.

Pamela owes a special debt of gratitude to Robert Clipsham, DVM, who helped her see the limitations of conventional Western veterinary medicine, and his veterinary technician, Vicky Rigdon, who first demonstrated to Pamela the efficacy of alternative medicines in a seemingly hopeless case. She also would like to thank Ketcham Chang, DVM, who allowed her to visit his veterinary clinic to see effective alternative medicine in action and who answered all questions patiently, no matter how uninformed. Pamela also owes a debt of gratitude to her parents, Raymond and Stella Leis, who encouraged her writing from childhood, and to Julie Rach, who introduced her to the wonderful world of writing books. To Phyllis and Lew, I luv U 2.

Dr. McCluggage would like to thank his many friends in the American Holistic Veterinary Medical Association and the International Veterinary Acupuncture Society, whose knowledge and help were instrumental in the development of his holistic skills.

Dr. McCluggage especially wants to point out to the reader that holistic medicine and holistic care of birds are primarily a state of mind. It is about acknowledging the bird as an individual with its own rights and needs.

Both authors share a special gratitude to all birds, without whom their lives would be less enjoyable.

1

A History of Bird Keeping

Bird keeping has a relatively short history, especially when compared to that of cats and dogs. Poems and other written accounts tell us that birds were kept in China several centuries ago by the ruling classes, among whom the Nightingale, or Pekin Robin, was especially prized for its song and beauty. We also know from written accounts that Falcons and Hawks have been valued in the Middle East for hundreds of years. They are still used there for hunting, especially by members of royal families.

Among the many legends about Alexander the Great is that he owned a parrot, a prized companion. He may also have brought parrots home to Greece from Asia, introducing bird keeping to Europe. The Alexandrine Parakeet, also called the Ring-necked Parakeet, a lovely medium-size parrot originating on the Indian subcontinent, was reportedly named after him.

During the height of the Roman Empire, some members of the nobility kept parrots as companion animals. It is unlikely that poorer members of society did so because buying and keeping these exotic animals would have been far out of their financial reach. Because of the proximity of Asia and Africa to Europe, it is believed that most of their pet birds initially came from these areas.

As fourteenth and fifteenth century European explorers began searching the seas for new and exotic discoveries, they brought home a variety of birds. A look at portraits of prosperous people during this time indicates that some, including King Henry VIII, kept birds as companion animals. In more recent times, one of Theodore Roosevelt's children kept a Hyacinth Macaw in the White House.

We don't know how well these people cared for their birds. We can deduce that they commonly did not meet the birds' physical or emotional needs because successful breeding of most captive bird species was a rarity until the twentieth century. As a rule, only birds that are emotionally and physically healthy will reproduce. Many bird owners simply bought a new wild-caught bird to replace a pet bird that had died. The supply of birds must have seemed endless.

For years zoos and serious aviculturists tried to breed many species, from finches to parrots, but were largely unsuccessful. Given that they were forced to rely on less-sophisticated methods for researching birds' needs than we have available today, their lack of success is less surprising than the occasional positive results.

More recently, massive education of the public through veterinary and bird-related publications has helped many people begin to realize that the supply of wild-caught birds is not limitless. It also made bird-lovers aware that domestic breeding programs were not only desirable for building a supply of pet birds but necessary to ensure the survival of species that had been decimated in their wild habitats.

More important to the survival of wild bird species, perhaps, was the 1992 Convention on International Trade in Endangered Species (CITES) that met in Japan. Agreements reached there resulted in restrictive laws on the exportation and importation of birds. With these laws in place, along with the cooperation of major international airlines, it has become difficult, and far more expensive, to buy most wild-caught birds than to buy a domestically bred, hand-fed, tame bird.

Proper nutrition remains a problem, however. There has been little progress in determining the basic nutritional needs of each species. Work continues in this area.

On the other hand, we are beginning to recognize that members of each bird species have distinct emotional needs. Those of us interested in birds observe our avian companions carefully to try to learn how we can meet those needs to help them live longer, happier lives than pet birds in years past. To do this, we have to learn to look at birds as more than beautiful accessories to our own lives.

BIRDS AS PETS

Birds are fascinating, intelligent pets. Because they are wild animals, they are far more complex than many other kinds of pets—dogs, for example. Dogs have been domesticated and bred to live as household pets for thousands of years. As pack animals they feel comfortable within an established, well-defined group hierarchy. A few relatively simple lessons in pack manners, training, for example, will help most owners understand how to keep a normal dog emotionally healthy and content.

On the other hand, even locally bred, hand-fed pet birds retain the instincts and emotional needs of their wild relatives. Domestically raised babies, especially members of the larger species, are only one or two generations away from their ancestors' native habitat. Because they retain these instincts for survival, these wonderful creatures are truly wild at heart.

To understand any bird, it is important to comprehend the finer points of avian interaction. Most birds kept as companion animals live in flocks in their natural habitat. Birds live in flocks for many reasons, including safety, emotional interaction and food gathering. A flock is a group of birds living together and usually comprised of one species, although there are a few instances in which two species may flock together. These are often small birds, such as Chickadees and Kinglets, that eat the same kind of food and may seek some degree of safety in larger, combined groups.

Within some flocks, one or two birds will act as watch birds, giving a warning when danger approaches. As soon as the other birds in the group hear the warning, they will settle in nearby trees or bushes and sit quietly until the danger has passed. Not only does a flock have more eyes and ears to look for predators than a single bird might, but a flock of flying birds can be distracting for a predator. Budgerigars, an Australian species called Parakeets in the United States, are a good example. Their ground color is green, which blends with the seed grasses they prefer to eat. The black and white stripes on a Budgie's head, neck and wings help break up the outline of the bird, making it difficult for a predator to see it. When flying in a flock, changing directions in undulating waves, they can be particularly difficult to track, especially for a predator looking for a single target.

Understanding flock behavior will give you many insights into the reasons for your pet bird's behavior. (Double Yellow-Head Amazon Parrots)

A flock of birds looking for food may find and communicate the location of food far more quickly than a single bird or a pair of birds can. A flock also supports its members emotionally through playing, feeding and grooming each other and caring for the young. Cockatoos, for example, will not leave a chick that falls out of a nest. Nor will they leave a flock member that has been wounded; they will come to the ground and stay near the wounded bird until it dies.

People who intend to keep a pet bird as a companion animal must be willing to learn from flock behavior and use the information to give their bird the kind of attention it needs to remain emotionally and physically healthy. If you bring the bird into your home, you become its flock and must commit yourself to supplying its physical and emotional needs to the best of your ability. To do this well, research the kind of bird you have or want to have.

Most Cockatoos, for instance, need close, hands-on care all day, every day. If you cannot give this kind of undivided attention to the Cockatoo, it will be miserable. The bird's screams, feather picking, self-mutilation, repetitive bouncing, circling the cage on the bars and other obsessive behavior will make you at least as unhappy as it is. A flock of Cockatoos, after all, would have given this bird exactly the kind of attention it craves.

On the other hand, some birds do not like petting. If you want close physical contact with the bird, spend time with it. During that time, let the bird show you what it wants and how it wants to be handled. Use this technique after you bring your bird home. Each bird is an individual, and it is essential that you respect its wishes. Often, small birds avoid close contact with humans. These birds will enjoy a large aviary with members of their own species.

It may surprise you to know that some large birds do not like to be handled and may bite if you try to pet them. The reasons for this behavior vary, but may include a lack of mutual preening among the species, as in Eclectus. Other large birds that don't like petting might have been mistreated, or they simply may not have had enough time to decide whether you are trustworthy for such an intimate bonding activity. In this setting, the bird can enjoy a life similar to that of its wild relatives. A good rule of thumb is to let the bird decide the amount and kind of attention it wants from you.

Parrots need to chew and destroy their surroundings. Wild parrots do this incessantly; it helps keep their beaks healthy, sharp and ready for use. Keeping a parrot obligates the owner to supply toys that the bird can chew. It also means the owner must understand that, when the bird chews a telephone cord, a computer cable, a door or a window frame, the responsibility lies with the owner, not the bird. The bird is doing what comes naturally.

For people who are willing to learn about and understand flock behavior and who want to fulfill the needs of the bird, living with a bird can bring great joy. For people who simply do not have the time or the interest, living with a bird can be difficult for both bird and owner.

2
HOLISTIC HEALTH CARE

Long before conventional Western medicine began to dominate the health-care field caregivers focused on the body's ability to heal itself. Hippocrates (468 to 377 B.C.), one of recorded history's first physicians, believed the job of practitioners was to help nature and to avoid injuring the patient.

In the years before and after Hippocrates, people in every culture worldwide sought ways to help people remain healthy; they battled disease and injury with whatever means they had available. Inevitably, disagreements occurred among medical practitioners. These conflicts often were between practitioners who followed the widely accepted theories of the day and those who ventured further afield for other possibilities. In nineteenth century Europe, for example, university-educated doctors were commonly referred to as regulars, while all other practitioners were called irregulars. A high rate of success with patients did not necessarily earn an irregular the respect of the regulars, nor did members of the status quo follow the ideas of irregulars, no matter the cost to their patients.

Samuel Thompson, a root and herb doctor in the United States in the early to mid-nineteenth century (an irregular), believed that illness resulted from a loss of natural balance in the body. He concluded that, if balance were restored with the use of herbal remedies, the body could regain the strength to heal itself. He wrote about the effectiveness of his methods during an 1805 yellow-fever epidemic. He noted that he lost none of the yellow-fever patients he had treated with herbs, while regular physicians lost half of the patients treated with conventional methods of the day.

The battle did not end there, of course. Today, many trained medical caregivers work to gain broader acceptance of holistic care in the United States, but it remains as difficult for them as it did for Thompson and his predecessors. One of the best known is Dr. Andrew Weil, who refers to holistic medicine as integrated medicine.

Weil is a Harvard-trained medical doctor. Following his graduation from medical school, he searched the South American jungles for miracle cures. Failing to find any that met his expectations, Weil returned to this country to reassess his approach to medical care. He now speaks passionately against the misuse of vaccines and antibiotics, but does not oppose their use in legitimate circumstances. He urges the medical community and the public to strengthen the body's healing capability to maintain or regain optimum health.

Weil, along with others who share his beliefs, wants the medical community and the public to learn to use vaccines and antibiotics properly and to have only reasonable expectations of their benefits. Holistic veterinarians have recognized the harm done by yearly vaccine programs for animals and have led the battle to stop the practice. Once given, a vaccine against a virus would be expected to last for the life of the animal. No scientific studies have shown that the effects of the vaccine became inactive after a year. Veterinary medicine is now beginning to move away from recommendations for yearly vaccines.

Antibiotics, developed largely in the twentieth century, can be potent treatments for many bacterial illnesses. Seen initially as miracle cures, their use ushered in an age in which patients began to expect to receive antibiotics for any disease. Doctors promoted this misuse of antibiotics by prescribing them for every illness to provide a cover in case the patient contracted a secondary bacterial infection. In fact, antibiotics are now commonly used against viral infections for which they are completely ineffective.

Conventional Western medicine estimates that as many as 80 percent of the prescriptions for antibiotics are unnecessary. Bacteria have become resistant to most antibiotics because of the overuse and abuse of these drugs.

The term "super bacteria" has entered our vocabulary as way to describe bacteria that should respond to antibiotics but do not. Diseases that were once thought to be easily treatable, and in some cases seemed to have been eradicated, have come back in forms so resistant to modern therapies that they threaten to cause epidemics again.

As people became reliant on antibiotics, they began to demand them for their pets, too, even when the pet suffered the effects of a viral disease. Avian medicine has seen similar problems emerge. Previously effective antibiotics no longer work.

In the 1980s and 1990s, a number of noted veterinarians began to look for alternative ways to care for animals. They wanted to avoid methods that depend solely on the use of antibiotics. Just as Weil sought to teach us to integrate and use all valid medical information, these veterinarians began sharing information about holistic care with each other and with their clients. They also began to teach the reasoning behind the alternative approaches. Among these veterinarians are several noted avian veterinarians who have experienced the limitations of using only conventional Western medicine to treat birds.

SAY THAT AGAIN? DEFINING TERMS

Numerous methods are available to keep our birds in good health and to help heal them when they are sick. Because so many alternative methods are not harmful in the hands of educated users, pet owners can use them as well as veterinarians. To add to your understanding of holistic care, here are some definitions of terms used throughout this book.

Holistic care: *The central idea is that your bird is an individual with physical and emotional needs and has a right to have those needs acknowledged and met. Also central to the beliefs of people who practice holistic care is the idea that the body does the healing, not the veterinarian or other practitioner. The caregiver aids the healing process using the least invasive methods possible. A holistic healer can be a veterinarian or an educated caregiver.*

To keep the bird healthy, a caregiver must constantly evaluate the bird's physical and emotional state in relation to the bird's environment. Meeting these needs will help keep the bird's stress level low. This helps it ward off disease or heal various parts of the body that may have been harmed physically.

When a bird becomes ill, a holistic healer views all of the bird's symptoms together, defining disease as the sum of all symptoms. The healer then evaluates the bird's symptoms

The premise of holistic care is that every bird is an individual with particular needs, all of which must be acknowledged and met for optimum health. (Gouldian Finch)

in relation to its environment to develop a therapeutic plan to help the bird begin to regain, and then maintain, its health. If the bird plucks its feathers, for instance, the healer looks at all other symptoms: its environment, its emotions, past and present illnesses, species variations and the needs and abilities of its human companion. The healer then must determine which signs are most significant to the case and what therapies will be most helpful.

The healer must also look at the physical and emotional needs of the species as well as the individual's personality and environment, both past and present. If the feather-plucking, screaming, cowering bird is a Lovebird, for example, the healer would understand that these birds are often social and need a great deal of attention, toys to play with and enough space to fly. They generally need a regularly scheduled period outside the cage each day to expend their tremendous energy and curiosity.

Cowering might indicate fear, which is unusual in this feisty species but perhaps not to this individual. To properly evaluate the underlying cause of the fear, the healer must observe the bird or talk to a perceptive owner to learn why the bird might feel threatened. Perhaps a large, aggressive cat now lives in the home, or maybe a man with a loud voice and unreserved mannerisms has moved into the house with the bird and its formerly single, quiet female owner. Such a drastic change in the environment might result in altered behavior and health in an avian companion.

In contrast to conventional Western medicine, holistic care emphasizes the individual variations of the disease picture. With diabetes, for example, all affected birds will show sugar spilling into the urine and increased thirst. Each individual bird, however, will have a unique set of outward signs of illness. Some birds will be obese, others will show weight loss, some will have secondary liver problems, and others will have intestinal problems.

Holistic care is not a quick fix. Generally, a new health-care focus is necessary—abandoning speed as a goal and working toward lasting health. The caregiver is a major partner in successful holistic care. That person must observe the bird carefully and use available knowledge to help the bird. When a bird is sick, it did not get in that state overnight. Unlike relieving symptoms, returning a degree of balance to the bird's body and restoring its vitality to the point where it can maintain its health takes time and patience on the part of the caregiver.

Conventional Western medicine: *This is the form of medical care practiced predominately in the Western world. It uses a diagnosis-driven system and lumps all illnesses into predefined disease names. Western medicine believes it can better define effective therapy by using the same medicines on each individual. In large part, practitioners direct therapy toward reducing or eliminating symptoms. If there is a fever, give aspirin; if there is a cough, give a cough suppressant.*

If you bring a bird suffering from a bacterial infection to a veterinarian who practices strictly conventional Western medicine, the veterinarian might take a culture of the droppings. The sample will be tested at a lab to determine what bacteria are present and to test various antibiotics against the bacteria found to try to predict which antibiotic will be most effective. This process takes several days. Until the culture comes back, the veterinarian may give the bird a broad-spectrum antibiotic, one viewed as being generally effective in alleviating a wide variety of symptoms similar to those displayed by the sick bird.

When the culture comes back, the veterinarian will check to see whether the prescribed antibiotic is listed as effective against that particular bacteria. If it is, the caregiver will be instructed to continue the treatment regimen. If not, the veterinarian will ask the caregiver to switch to one that was effective at killing the bacteria under laboratory conditions. If all goes well, the infection will go away over the course of ten days to two weeks. As some bird owners know, however, many birds that become sick for the first time seem to relapse later or develop new illnesses. Herein lies the problem: Although conventional medicine often is efficient at eliminating symptoms, it does not seek out the true disease, and no therapy is directed at helping the bird heal itself.

It may surprise you to know that a holistic avian veterinarian would have treated the bird in some parallel ways but would have gone further. In this case, the holistic veterinarian might have done the culture and prescribed the appropriate antibiotic, if necessary. However, the treatment would not have stopped there. This veterinarian would have evaluated the bird according to holistic standards. The holistic doctor might have also advocated the use of a remedy known to strengthen the bird's body or an herb known to help heal the liver, if it was involved in the disease. The doctor would advise about any appropriate changes to diet and environment. This method would help the bird heal itself and would render it more capable of fighting subsequent illnesses without further antibiotics. Not only would the bird be symptom free, it may become healthier than ever before.

Pharmaceutical medicine: *These chemically altered compounds are unlike any found in nature. Practitioners of conventional Western medicine use them to dramatically alter biochemical functions of the body. These compounds often have side effects and can be quite toxic at only slightly larger doses than what is prescribed as the effective dose. Two aspirins are fine, for example, but six aspirins will cause illness.*

Allopathic medicine: *This term is sometimes used interchangeably with conventional Western medicine, although this is not strictly accurate. Allopathic medicine is defined as a system of medicine that uses drugs to treat symptoms. The symptoms being treated are dissimilar to or the opposite of the effects of the drug being given. If there is a fever, allopathic medicine lowers the fever with aspirin. Holistic medicine, especially homeopathy, often tries to subtly strengthen the disease symptoms, believing that the body's symptoms are its way to heal itself. It involves the use of procedures that can relieve symptoms of a disease.*

Allopathic medicine concentrates on symptoms and their relief. It does not treat the root of the disease. Generally, allopathic medicine uses invasive techniques such as antibiotics, pharmaceuticals, vaccines and surgery, which can have serious side effects. Alternative medicine uses a less invasive, gentler approach to healing.

Alternative medicine: *This is a collection of methods used to help restore a patient to health. It also refers to ways in which a caregiver can help the bird (or other animal, including a human) maintain good health. Effective health-care methods that do not fit the distinctive nature of conventional Western medicine may be grouped under this term.*

Every living entity has a vital force within. To maintain long-lasting health, the entity (or body) must be in balance. To determine what remedy will help return a bird's body to balance, the veterinarian or caregiver must evaluate each bird as an individual. This recognizes that, although the bird is a member of a species with certain overall characteristics, it is as much an individual as each human is. Consequently, the caregiver must take into account and evaluate the bird's unique personality, environment, diet, age and preferences to put together as accurate a picture of this bird as possible. This is a time-consuming and difficult process, but the alternative caregiver is working toward a long-range goal—that the bird will remain healthy and happy for the long term. Some alternative therapies include acupuncture and aquapressure, Reiki, traditional Chinese medicine, herbal or botanical medicines, Chinese herbal medicine, homeopathic medicine, nutraceutical medicine and nutritional therapy.

Traditional Chinese medicine: *This type of medicine (TCM) looks for and attempts to maintain balance in the body and strives for equilibrium between yin and yang. According to this school of thought, the body contains a passive, cold, quiet state called yin and an aggressive, hot, active state called yang. When the two states become unbalanced, the body develops disease. TCM stresses that yin and yang exist not only in the body but also in the environment, although nothing is totally yin or exclusively yang. By learning to look at the world, our animal companions and ourselves, we can acquire the ability to make healthful decisions about our lives. If the bird becomes agitated, for example, we can use this elegantly simple theory as part of the decision-making, problem-solving process. This would cause us to speak calmly to the bird to help it regain a more tranquil state of mind. This theory rejects aggression as a solution to any problem. By hitting or shouting at the bird, we simply deepen the bird's aggressive feelings and ensure a continuation of its belligerent behavior.*

Acupuncture: *Because of their fast metabolic rate, it is believed that birds are more responsive to acupuncture than mammals. An acupuncturist simply inserts sterile, stainless-steel needles only a few millimeters deep at prescribed acupuncture points, which are known to have various effects on the body. If possible, the needles remain in the bird's body for five to fifteen minutes. The needles are turned once during treatment. This is not a painful procedure.*

Generally, a veterinarian or other certified acupuncturist should carry out this treatment. It is important to the bird's well-being and the success of the treatment, however, for the bird's human companion to understand the technique and remain with the bird to provide emotional support during treatment.

In this form of treatment, a practitioner stimulates specific points on the bird's body using acupuncture needles, moxibustion sticks, injections, low-level lasers or magnets. The

American Veterinary Medical Association (AVMA) considers it an integral part of veterinary medicine.

Acupuncture is an old technique believed to have been developed in China. Records of it have been found on bone etchings dating to 1600 B.C. It is hypothesized that acupuncture strengthens the body's vital force, called the Qi or Chi, allowing the body to restore its natural, internal balance.

There is no valid reason to fear the spread of disease by acupuncture. Reputable, knowledgeable practitioners use steel needles made specifically for their intended purpose. These needles are disposable and are used only once.

Acupuncture is not suitable for all birds. Most would rather pull out the needles than let them sit. A bird's natural compulsion is to remove any foreign object from itself or its companions during normal preening. If the bird seems unlikely to sit quietly or to allow the needles to remain in position, several variations can be employed. The needles may be left in for only a few seconds, rotated and then removed.

Alternatively, vitamin B_{12} can be injected into the acupuncture points, simulating the same pressure that is applied using a needle. This is sometimes called aquapuncture. Vitamin B_{12} is completely nontoxic and remains at the site of the acupuncture point for a few minutes, maintaining pressure at the point. This provides the same effect as with needles only without restraining the bird. Aquapuncture is as painless as needle insertion.

Reiki: *This form of touch therapy (pronounced ray-key) helps the body heal both physically and mentally. Although a holistic veterinarian may use this technique on your bird initially, you can learn to do it as well.*

Reiki is an ancient method of healing using positive energy. Every living thing has energy, and when a plant or animal dies, the energy is transformed from one state of existence to another. This energy consists of both positive and negative forms. Practitioners of Reiki allow themselves to act as conduits for positive energy (also called universal life-giving energy) and love to pass through them into the animal they are stroking.

Although touch therapy has been reviled by some medical caregivers until recently, more physicians and veterinarians now recognize the value of touch as a part of overall treatment plans. In diseases as catastrophic as AIDS and cancer in humans or Psittacine Beak and Feather Disease in birds (as well as for more minor illnesses or injuries), handling by a caring individual reduces stress and helps restore the body's balance.

To realize the potential of touch therapy in the treatment of birds, we need only to look at flock behavior. Birds constantly touch each other. Even birds that do not preen each other, such as Eclectus Parrots, sit closely together, touch and bonk each other's beaks and feed each other. Touch is important to all birds; it is one way of conveying love. An isolated bird, like other sequestered animals, will fail to thrive and will die.

Various bird behaviors, including preening, indicate the importance of touch.

Herbal and botanical medicine: *This form of therapy uses plants and plant products in treatment strategies. Herbal medicine is the single most popular form of medicine throughout the world today. A remarkably large body of research proves its effectiveness. Although proponents of conventional Western medicine once renounced herbal medicine, there has been increased interest in herbal therapies in the Western world during the past twenty years. As herbal therapies become more accepted for human use, pet owners have begun to demand them for their companion animals, too.*

Chinese herbal medicine: *Practitioners of Chinese herbal medicine have studied herbs and their effects on the body for centuries. Because of the long-term research done in Asia, the effects of many herbs on the body are well known. Although some people believe that Chinese herbs are more potent than Western herbs, we do not agree. All herbs can be highly effective if used appropriately. This book will help readers learn to use some herbs to treat their birds safely and effectively for specific conditions.*

Homeopathic medicine: *According to the World Health Organization, homeopathy is the second most popular form of health medicine in the world today, surpassing conventional Western medicine. (Herbal medicine is the most popular.)*

Samuel Hahneman, a German physician, developed homeopathy more than two hundred years ago. The name comes from two words: homeo, *which means resembling or similar to, and* pathos, *which means disease. Homeopathy is the treatment of disease with medicines that would create symptoms similar to the disease if given to healthy animals. This is called the law of similars:* Like cures like.

Although the concept had been used in various cultures for centuries prior to his research, Hahneman refined it. He noticed that his patients got almost as sick from the treatment as from the illness. His major contribution to this approach was to dilute the remedies. He then shook the dilution, called *successing* the remedy. This made it a more powerful agent against the illness. Homeopathic drugs are usually administered in highly dilute, minute doses.

As in other alternative methods, homeopathy views the animal as a whole, not just as symptoms of illness: The entire animal suffers from the disease. To correctly determine which remedy would help the affected animal, the practitioner discusses the bird's emotional symptoms as well as the signs of illness with the caregiver.

Homeopathic remedies stimulate the animal's vital force, giving it the renewed ability to heal itself. Although these remedies, like other alternative therapies, act slowly, they can produce long-term results. A bird that has chronic sinus infections, for instance, can be treated with antibiotics, which will achieve quick but short-lived results. A bird dosed with homeopathic remedies will, with time, become free of this difficult kind of infection.

Homeopathy works especially well with birds that respond well to energetic therapeutics. We believe that homeopathy is the strongest form of energetic medicine. It is preferred to use *classic homeopathy* with birds, the use of only one remedy at a time. Combining homeopathic medications will help birds, but will not achieve the deep healing of single remedies.

It is strongly recommend that you take a seriously ill bird for an examination with an avian veterinarian—Western medicine could save its life. For mild illnesses or to strengthen the bird after Western medical therapies are used, a homeopath can be consulted. The homeopath can then treat the bird with the appropriate homeopathic remedies for long-term health.

It is extremely important for caregivers to understand their birds' physical and emotional needs. Only with this kind of insight can you know when your bird is stressed and in need of help. This is especially important for birds, which tend to hide all obvious signs of illness until they are practically beyond help. This instinctive behavior helps them avoid attracting the attention of a predator in the wild. On the other hand, the lack of overt signs can confuse uneducated owners and may cause them to lose their birds to preventable or curable illnesses.

Nutraceutical medicine: *This is one of the newer branches of the holistic therapies, evolving over the last thirty years. The term comes from a combination of the words "nutrition" and "pharmaceuticals." Nutraceuticals are the purified, chemically isolated compounds of natural substances. Because these compounds can be produced in concentrated forms, they can be administered in doses larger than the body normally has to deal with. In this form of therapy, a patient might be given aloe vera, astragalus, calendula, chamomile, echinacea or evening primrose. This book will guide you in the use of nutraceuticals.*

Nutritional therapy: *This is the practice of using food or food products, such as vitamins, oils and amino acids, in an attempt to cure disease. It can involve feeding foods to change certain body* *functions, such as the immune system's response to disease. Some people divide nutritional therapy into nutritional medicine, which includes food extracts or isolated compounds, and food therapy, which uses whole foods.*

THE CHANGING TIDE

It's difficult to swim against the tide, even when it means doing something you know is right that might differ from mainstream thinking on the subject. For many years, the majority opinion about outstanding veterinary care stood staunchly with conventional Western medicine. In the mid-1980s, however, evidence mounted steadily that conventional methods alone often fail to offer the quality of care animals deserve. These methods frequently offer a quick elimination of symptoms but do not return an animal to long-term health. Looking for better treatment for animals, some veterinarians began exploring holistic methods to use in conjunction with conventional treatments.

Not all avian veterinarians are convinced of the merits of the holistic approach, however. As with any approach to medical care, whether old or new, holistic medical care has detractors. Most often, a detractor will say that alternative methods simply produce a placebo effect. This means that an alternative therapy convinces the animal's mind that the therapy will heal the body, even if the therapy is as innocuous as spring water.

People who use holistic methods believe this argument proves their point. Holistic caregivers acknowledge the body's ability to heal itself. They view their part in the process as being similar to a coach. They guide and aid the process of achieving balance in the body so it can get back to a normal, healthy state and can work as intended.

In July 1996, the American Veterinary Medical Association issued guidelines for the use of alternative therapies and acknowledged the effectiveness of these therapies when used correctly. This conservative group finally recognized what the rest of the world has always acknowledged, though it did so under pressure. The AVMA describes holistic veterinary medicine as a comprehensive approach to health care that employs alternative and conventional diagnostic and therapeutic modalities. It incorporates, but is not limited to, the principles of acupuncture and acutherapy, botanical medicine, chiropractic, homeopathy, massage therapy, nutraceuticals and physical therapy as well as conventional medicine, surgery and dentistry.

BUT WILL IT WORK WITH BIRDS?

Birds are good subjects for holistic health care because of their emotional and physical composition. Unlike many other animals, especially those that have been domesticated, birds may hide signs of illness.

People often view life in the wild as cruel, but it is, above all, practical. Each animal has to eat to live. Carnivores must eat meat to survive. A predator needs to expend the smallest amount of energy possible to capture its prey. This helps the predatory animal maintain the strength to survive until it can find, catch and keep its next meal long enough to eat it. The predator must often do this without becoming prey itself to a larger or fiercer animal. This is not always an easy task. To accomplish it, predators tend to prey on the most vulnerable, sick, young and helpless animals.

Birds understand this predator-prey relationship instinctively. When the bird feels sick or becomes injured, it will hide overt signs of trouble as long as it can. If a wild bird appears weakened, the flock may force it to leave the group for the safety of the majority, or the sick bird may simply lag behind the flock because it has no energy. Try as it might to hide its symptoms, a sick bird will show you signs of illness early in the disease process. The signs will be subtle but, as a trained observer, you will see them.

Changes in behavior are often early signs of illness. Your bird may be grumpier than in the past. Perhaps it will want to stay in its cage more than before. An uneducated care-giver might miss subtle clues the bird cannot help but give. Look for these early signs of illness and act soon. By the time your bird sits fluffed on the bottom of its cage, it may be desperately ill.

Holistic care means, in part, viewing companion birds as whole, living, feeling, thinking creatures. Carefully observe what is normal each day so you can spot any change in physical or emotional behavior as soon as it occurs. This approach will help you notice the first, subtle signs of illness. You then can make an educated evaluation and help your bird regain its health.

It is important to learn how to evaluate your bird's needs *before* it becomes ill. Providing the proper amount and kind of attention for your bird's personality, altering your environment to suit your bird's needs and feeding it a nutritious diet can help its body fight illness and can keep your bird healthy for a long time.

3

THE EMOTIONAL BIRD

Although birds have been kept as pets in many cultures for hundreds of years, they are not domesticated. Until the 1992 CITES (Convention on International Trade in Endangered Species) law forbade the exportation of parrots, almost all birds were wild-caught. To domesticate an animal takes hundreds of years, specifically breeding the animal for behavioral traits that we recognize in other domestic animals. A good example of a domesticated animal is the dog. These animals have been companions to humans for hundreds of thousands of years. They were bred for specific purposes such as herding, pulling loads and hunting. Centuries of observation have led us to believe that we can predict canine behavior with a high degree of accuracy. Birds do not have this type of domestic breeding history. Hand-fed birds cannot be considered domesticated either. Although tamer than wild-caught birds, they do not come from long lines of domestically bred birds.

BIRD BRAINS

People who live with companion birds or who watch wild birds know that birds are intelligent animals. Wild birds must think creatively to survive in the wild. They always are on the lookout for food and water while at the same time avoiding predators. This involves not only on-the-spot thinking but also planning, which humans view as a sign of intelligence.

Over the years, researchers have used Crows, Pigeons and Canaries (among other birds) to test avian intelligence. At Harvard, investigators found that Pigeons can extend the idea of "human" to both males and females and to all races, cultures, chronological ages and sizes. They can also relate parts of the human body to people and can differentiate between man-made and natural. At Brown University, psychologists found that laboratory Pigeons can learn to recognize each letter of the alphabet.

In 1981, Dr. Irene Pepperberg, now affiliated with the University of Arizona in Tucson, published a research paper on avian intelligence. Her subject was Alex, an African Grey parrot she bought at a pet store for about $700. Alex understands direct commands and responds to them appropriately about 80 percent of the time. He differentiates between concepts as complex as size, color and shape and responds with an appropriate word or phrase. He refers correctly to his special foods, all of the objects in his environment that play a roll in his life, such as his gym, the shower and about a hundred other things. He sometimes refuses a request by saying "No." He also tells experimenters what to do: "Go away," "Go pick up the cup," "Come here." At this point, Pepperberg is teaching Alex to read.

EMOTIONS AND RESPONSE

All animals have a fight-or-flight response. This life-saving, instinctive reaction is built in to save our lives. When something physical or emotional startles us or threatens us, adrenaline is released. This gives us the capability either to flee faster than we would otherwise or to stand and fight with greater strength than we would normally have. Small-boned, terrified mothers have lifted cars off their children and have beaten off attackers far larger than themselves. As positive as this fight-or-flight response is, it can also be destructive if it is induced frequently in the bird—something that happens in many homes.

All animals respond to danger with this fight or flight reaction. The danger does not have to be real; perceived danger causes the same response. A companion bird has the same physical and emotional structure as its wild relatives. It will be afraid of many of the same things as the wild bird including much of what happens in a home. When a companion bird perceives threat, however, it often cannot respond appropriately—either flying away from or fighting the danger—because it is caged or has had its wings trimmed. This often increases its fears. At the very least, it may cause adverse effects. Think about yourself and how often you have developed a cold when you were stressed out.

EMOTIONS AND HEALTH

We know from practical experience and from scientific research that emotions affect the state of an animal's health, whether the animal is a human being or a bird. The more intelligent an animal is, the keener its perception of danger and the greater its stress.

Stress diminishes an animal's ability to fight disease. An emotionally healthy companion bird, no matter the species, exhibits signs of emotional contentment. It eats well and sleeps restfully, and it plays with toys or interacts with its caregiver and/or flock mates in ways it feels comfortable. A common Budgie (also called a Budgerigar or a Parakeet) is remarkably active throughout its day. It runs around, plays, chews things and, in general, finds lots of ways to get into trouble. A Budgie that is not emotionally secure and happy often just sits in its cage doing little throughout the day.

Children are often troublesome for birds. Children move rapidly and abruptly and have little understanding of the need to give the bird its space so the bird can determine what is wanted of it. Children are also uncertain in their interaction with the bird, and this uncertainty is often transferred to the bird.

Many birds are flocking animals and have a close, intimate relationship with the entire flock. Small birds rarely expose themselves to areas such as the open sky or the ground where they might be attacked by predators. They flit from branch to branch in search of food and wary of danger at all times. They tend to eat grass seeds as well as some insects. They consider all larger animals a danger. Understanding the behaviors our companion birds would have in the wild can help us adjust their captive environment to keep them healthier.

The Cockatoo is a flock-oriented bird that needs close companionship to survive.

Flocking birds are often happiest in a group, even in captivity. Knowing that they are often afraid of larger animals such as dogs, cats and humans, we can see that it would be a good idea to place a Finch or Cockatiel cage near a wall and out of the center of activity. If you keep a small flock of birds in the same cage, don't place several different species in the same cage or aviary. In most situations, only one species per cage or aviary is appropriate.

Because wild birds of these species like bushes and trees, placing nontoxic house-plants near their cage gives them a sense of security. For the birds' sense of well-being, provide a cage large enough for them to fly from end to end and to perch without crowding. As in a wild flock, your Canary or Finch flock should contain males and females.

Other birds have different requirements. It is your responsibility to learn whether your bird is social or more independent and whether it lives peacefully with other bird species. Lovebirds and Quaker Parakeets, for example, are aggressive, territorial animals and may kill more reclusive birds, even if they are physically larger. A Toucan may eat a small-er bird such as a Budgie or a Canary. In the wild, this would be acceptable, necessary behav-ior. You cannot alter the behavior, so you must create an environment that will work with your bird's instincts.

You, as the caregiver, have the ultimate responsibility for noting the causes of stress in your bird's life. We can give you general guidelines for things that can stress your bird. We can also tell you what you can do to help your bird's emotional health. Each bird, how-ever, is a unique individual that needs your keen observation and insights into your unique environment to give it the stress-free home it needs.

STRESSORS IN THE ENVIRONMENT

FOOD

Nutrition is necessary for survival. If an animal does not have enough food or the correct kind of food, it cannot survive. Research about the exact food needed for the optimum health of each species has not been done. At present, we can only approximate the nutri-tional needs of each species.

There are basic nutritional practices we can follow, however, to avoid stressing our birds. If the bird was hand-raised and weaned on certain foods or learned to view a food as normal at the pet store, breeder's facility or a former home, you should continue to offer this food along with others when you attempt to balance the bird's diet. Eliminating a "comfort food," as long as it is not toxic, to replace it with a more healthful food can be stressful if done suddenly.

Birds adapt to new diets slowly. This helps them survive in the wild. A wild bird that readily eats strange food may die from eating something poisonous. Introduce all new foods gradually with other foods. Allow the bird to watch you eat the food. Birds can learn by example, but the understanding will develop slowly. The process of changing the bird's diet from all seeds to one that includes fruits, vegetables and some protein sources may take a long time. Teaching the bird to eat healthful food, however, is worth the effort.

A diet modification plan for your bird might take six months or longer. Take your time. You should never try to starve your bird into eating new foods. Feed the foods it likes once daily; offer such a small amount that your bird will have finished eating it about halfway through the day. Making sure there is no food in the cage for several hours before the next meal will make your bird hungry enough to "forage" for new foods.

Routinely monitoring your bird's weight is important because weight loss is often one of the earliest signs of illness. Scales with perches attached make it easy and stress free to do this. Keep records of your bird's weight and eating habits. Loss of appetite and a resulting drop in weight can be an early sign of illness.

Your bird may choose not to eat certain foods, no matter what you do or how you present them. If this is the case, offer another food that has similar nutrients. If your bird refuses carrots, for example, offer yams or pumpkin.

Always feed your bird at the same times every day. Imagine yourself in a bed, unable to get up. If you depended on someone to bring your meals, you might become frantic if you could not communicate and could not get the food yourself. Your bird may experience this same sense of panic if you fail to develop and maintain a timetable. Wild birds eat soon after the sun rises, and then chow down again in the evening before they roost for the night. Chapter 6, "Nutrition," gives you a reasonable feeding schedule to follow.

WATER

It must be plentiful and clean and must look like something the bird wants to drink. If you add liquid vitamins or foul-tasting supplements, your bird may refuse it. This will stress your bird physically and emotionally. To keep the water clean, position the water bowl off the floor and never under a perch from which the bird might defecate. Some birds adapt well to water bottles. Never remove the water container the bird is used to, however, until you are sure the bird uses the bottle regularly. Be sure to check the bottle every day to make sure it is still working. Whether you use a bowl or water bottle, you should change the water twice daily.

THE BIRD'S HOUSE

We've come a long way with housing for birds. We now know that the bird must live in a cage large enough to allow it to spread its wings and fly. Small birds should be able to fly from one end of the cage to another without hindrance. Avoid cages with lead or zinc because they are toxic and can kill your bird. Avoid cages with small spaces in which birds might catch their nails, feet, legs, beaks or wings.

Before you put more than one bird in a cage, make sure they get along. It's best to house birds of the same species together. Never overcrowd a cage. Birds have a natural instinct for how much food and space there is to divide among a group.

Buy perches of varying sizes for the cage to approximate perching conditions in the wild. You can find manzanita branches in most pet stores—these make good perches and interesting chewing material. The perch should be large enough that the bird's foot does not quite enclose it at its smallest part. Avoid sandpaper covers for perches because they can rub sore places on the bird's feet. Place perches logically so they do not prevent small birds from flying end to end in their cage. For larger birds, locate the perches so your pet can flex and stretch its wings. Refrain from placing perches over food, water or bathing dishes to avoid contamination with urine and feces.

Your bird will treat its cage as its territory, and you must respect this attitude. It reflects a necessary instinct for protecting the area in which a flock finds food and shelter. If you reach into your bird's cage, your bird may bite. You should expect and respect this. Allow the bird to come out on its own and learn to read the physical signs your bird will send to let you know when or if it is acceptable to reach into the cage.

Cage placement is very important. Put the cage in the room where you spend the most time, such as a family room. Locate it at the edge of the room, perhaps in a corner, to give your bird a sense of security. In that position, no one can approach the cage from the rear or sides to surprise the bird. You might also consider putting nontoxic plants around the back and at each end of the cage. The bird may chew the plants as it would in the wild. The most important consideration is how your bird views the location. Is your bird gregarious and eager to be with you constantly, or is it easily rattled by quick movement? If you have small children or large dogs, place the cage out of reach. Keep in mind that, if the bird bites a child, an adult or another animal, it is reacting appropriately to the situation as it perceives it. Help others in your home avoid behaving in ways the bird will think of as threatening.

Many companion birds fear being trapped in an exposed location, as when they are placed in a cage or on a perch in front of a clear glass window. They can see predatory birds in the sky, can observe flashes of light when sunlight bounces off windshields of passing cars or when lightning brightens the night sky, and they may watch as a cat stalks a bird outside.

Because they have no way to escape, they sit in a constant state of fear. In addition, sitting directly in front of a glass window may expose the bird to excessive heat when the sun shines on the window. This also is a poor practice from a security standpoint. If someone sees your bird and decides it is worth stealing, the person may come back to take your pet.

NOISE

In the wild, quiet indicates that a predator or something out of the ordinary is near. As soon as the intruder goes away, the noise level picks up. In your home, you can use music to help calm your bird. Keep soothing music playing even when you are away. A little experimentation will help you determine what kind of music your bird prefers. It often is whatever you listen to when you are home and happy, but don't assume that. Play various kinds of music and watch your bird's body language.

TEMPERATURE

Avoid extreme changes in temperature; they can stress the bird's body. Generally, place the bird's cage away from doors or windows (especially those you might open or that have no screens) and heat or air-conditioning ducts. Never put the cage in the kitchen or the bathroom. Both rooms are subject to abrupt temperature changes, and in either room, you are likely to use products with fumes toxic to your bird. Standing water, always a danger to birds, is often at hand in both rooms. Birds that fall into toilets, full sinks or pet water bowls may drown if they can't get out. Wet feathers and steep sides make it difficult for them to fly out of danger.

SLEEP

Wild birds generally wake up at dawn and spend the day hunting for food, playing, socializing and dodging predators. Around dusk, they find a safe perch and rest for the night, usually about ten hours. Rest is as important for your bird's well-being as it is for yours. To keep your bird emotionally and physically healthy, you must give it time to recharge its batteries. If you have the bird in the family room, turn off the television at a reasonable hour, turn off the light and leave the room. Some birds do well with a covered cage at night; others feel more secure without a cover. This enables them to see their surroundings.

It may be a good idea to plug in a low-light night light to prevent your bird from panicking at night. Some birds react too quickly to unusual sounds in the night and fly against the cage bars in an attempt to flee the perceived danger. A night light can give them a measure of comfort by letting them look at the source of the noise.

Listen at night for thrashing. If you hear it, you may want to use a night light right away. If the thrashing continues, look for the cause. Is a cat bothering the birds? Is the family dog wandering around the room? Maybe mice are scurrying around in the dark. In the 1980s at the Houston Zoo, the curator of birds found that the birds became frenzied at night. Closer inspection revealed the presence of rodents. Your bird will communicate the presence of a problem; you must do a bit of detective work to find out what the problem is.

SEX AND THE SINGLE BIRD

All animals have a sex drive, which ensures the survival of the species. With birds, both the males and females cycle sexually when they have reached sexual maturity. With sexual maturity come new behaviors that often surprise the caretaker. The bird may become territorial and guard its cage. It might start biting other people to drive them away from you. It might even start biting you to tell you to keep away from these other people, whom the bird views as a threat to the bonded relationship it has with you.

Over time, pet birds may become frustrated with life. They always are looking for that nest box but it never materializes. These frustrations can lead to problem behaviors, but they may also lead to stresses that eventually cause physical illness.

The need to breed may become strongest when a bird cycles reproductively once or twice each year.

Your bird might decide that one of its human caretakers will become its surrogate mate, or it might choose the cute bird it sees in a mirror. Some birds take toys as mates, jealously guarding this new companion. Whomever the bird chooses as its surrogate mate, consider the frustrations from the bird's point of view. It has a companion who will not mate, help it find a nest, build a nest and guard it as it would in the wild.

This deprivation and frustration may make the bird act out. Coping behaviors that sexually frustrated birds may develop include screaming, abnormal feather grooming (feather plucking), refusing to come out of the cage and play or destroying things in a desperate attempt to alleviate the bird's sexual feelings. The bird's system says go, but its "mate" says no.

This inability to mate is the cause of one of the most troublesome emotional problems we face with our birds. They can't be spayed or neutered, and there are no safe, effective, hormonal therapies that will help.

Understanding that normal sexual urges are leading to many of the abnormal or troublesome behaviors birds exhibit is the first step in helping them. It is important to be considerate of their frustrations and to help as much as we can to gently moderate their behaviors. Often, we just need to wait for them to complete the sexual cycle, which usually lasts about a month.

Some sexually frustrated birds develop serious behavioral problems or physical illnesses that cannot be ignored. Other sections of this book discuss some herbal, nutraceutical and acupuncture therapies that can reduce the problems of sexual frustration.

LOVE AND A SENSE OF BELONGING

As a flock animal, your bird needs constant reminders of your affection and a sense that it is an important member of your family. In the flock, each bird has a specific role or roles to fill and gets regular feedback from the other birds, which would reassure it. Pet birds need love and reassurance from their human caretakers. Some need constant, hands-on acknowledgment, while others may simply need to sit nearby as you carry on your daily routine.

Read several books on the species of bird you already have or want to buy to serve as a baseline in your search for the level and kind of attention your bird needs. It is then your job to supply that attention. The way you show your love is important; it must fit your bird's expectations and needs. Your goal as a holistic caretaker must be to meet your bird's needs and not try to mold those needs to your own requirements. If you have not bought the bird yet, think carefully about the match between your personality and what you know about a species. If you already own the bird, work to adapt your personality and time schedule to the bird's requirements.

SAY NO TO PUNISHMENT

Physical punishment has no part in a loving, trusting relationship between a bird and its caretaker. Hitting and throwing things at the bird to correct what you view as inappropriate behavior can only cause a rift between you and your pet by undermining the level of trust, perhaps permanently. Evaluate the behavior you feel is inappropriate.

You can change the environment to help the situation. If the bird has destroyed something valuable, you should either remove all valuable items from the bird's access or be prepared to be more observant. If the bird screams, look for reasons. Does it need more out-of-cage play time? Does it feel threatened by a cat, dog, child or misbehaving adult in your house? Realizing that you, as flock leader, must solve the problem is the first step in a holistic approach to finding a solution.

EDUCATING, NOT TRAINING

Those of us dedicated to holistic care recognize and want to emphasize that there is a major difference between training and educating. Training is what we hear about most. If your bird screams, trainers say to cover the cage. If the bird bites, trainers tell you to shake your hand until the bird falls off. Training is a system of rewards and punishments, positives and negatives. When you do things the way I want, there are no negative consequences. This demonstrates a hierarchy of authority: I am the boss, and you are not. Training becomes a demeaning process to both parties involved.

Educating an animal implies a cooperative activity, one that, in its essence, is a free and open two-way communication. It is a bonding between the caretaker and the animal in which the caretaker is as receptive to the animal's desires as the animal is to the caretaker's. It is essentially letting each other know what is okay and what is not okay for each other.

When you bring a new bird into your home, let it decide the time frame for learning to trust you. Talk to the bird constantly in a reassuring tone. It will watch you as you go about your day, and the fact that you are not demanding anything from the bird will reassure it. Accept the bird for what it is instead of attempting to make it into your idea of an ideal pet. You must learn about avian behavior and keep your expectations reasonable for the species and for the individual. Just as the bird learns about you, you should take the time to learn about the bird. While the bird sizes you up and tries to figure out what you want in the relationship, you should do the same thing. Does this bird want a close physical relationship and cuddling, or does it simply want the comfort of remaining in the same room? The bird should decide, not you. Why? You chose to bring the bird into your home; the bird was not able to make that decision. It is up to you to accommodate the bird's needs. Only then will it be a true companion and not just a pet.

The bird may learn to trust you in a day or two, or it may take months or years to fully develop a relationship. You know your intentions are good; the bird knows nothing of the sort. The bird may have memories of past mistreatment or extreme stress; you know nothing of that recollection.

Currently, a popular training tool is the command "Step up!" Trainers will tell you to repeat this command firmly as you put your hand in front of the bird. This, we concede, teaches the bird to get on your hand; however, it's unnecessary. Birds are intelligent animals. If you look at the bird and put your hand near it, the bird will step on if it seems like a safe and reasonable thing to do.

For a trusting companion bird, the verbal command is similar to someone hitting your arm to get your attention. It's annoying. The bird got the message that you wanted it to step up when you put your hand near its feet. If the bird refuses to get on, it has a reason. It then becomes your problem to find out why and to resolve the issue in your relationship. You need to fix your end of the two-way line of communication that must exist between you and your companion.

It is impossible to have a worthwhile relationship with a companion bird if the goal is to train it to our needs and desires. Truly satisfying relationships develop when we educate ourselves about the needs and desires of the bird and then use that knowledge to open up communication.

Ways to Establish Trust with a New or Frightened Bird

- Use a gentle touch and a soothing voice.
- Move slowly and steadily when you handle the bird.
- Avoid startling the bird. Announce yourself by talking quietly as you come into a room or when approaching the bird's cage.
- Remain mindful of the bird's likely reactions to new objects and situations.
- Remember that the noise level in your home and sounds you and your family consider normal might startle your new companion. These sounds include appliances, people and other household pets.
- Be patient.
- Open your heart and communicate through love.

4

THE PHYSICAL BIRD

In many ways, birds are unique among animals. They are the only animal with feathers. Most birds can fly, and only insects and bats can match that feat. Birds lay eggs to reproduce and care for their young. Birds live in all climates and on all continents.

To care for these wonderful creatures properly, it is important for bird owners and other caregivers to understand how birds' bodies work.

AVIAN ANATOMY

There are six external parts of a bird: the head, neck, trunk, tail, wing and pelvic limb. The head includes the forehead, the crown, the back of the head, the beak, the nostrils, the eye and ear openings, the lore (the area between the eye and beak), the throat and the cheek. Neck length varies by species. It must be long enough for the bird to groom properly by reaching the uropygial gland near the base of the bird's tail and to perform other tasks typical of the species such as finding food, watching for danger and nest building.

The bird's trunk is located between the neck and the tail. The trunk comprises the thorax, the abdomen and the pelvis. The top part of the trunk consists of the back

Birds such as Macaws that fly long distances have long wings for soaring. (Blue and Gold Macaw)

(nearest the neck) and the rump (nearest the tail). The breast, the belly and the region under the tail are parts of the underbody of the bird.

The tail is comprised of overlapping pairs of flight feathers called retrices. Under the retrices are smaller coverts (in most species except the Peacock) that cover the base of the retrices.

The wing consists of primary and secondary flight feathers, or remiges, and smaller covert feathers lying on top of the longer flight feathers. There are four wing shapes: elliptical, broad soaring, long soaring and high speed. These shapes developed over many years, adapting to the needs of the species. Birds that must travel over long distances such as oceans, for instance, have long wings for soaring.

Bird feet have adapted to the habitat and feeding needs of each species. The foot of most bird species has four toes, although some have fewer. The arrangement of the toes also varies by family or species. Songbirds have three toes pointing forward and one pointing backward—an arrangement well-suited to perching—with the back toe used for grasping. Passerines such as Manikins, Canaries, Finches, Starlings and Mynahs, to name only a few, have this type of feet. A parrot's foot has two toes that point forward and two that point backward, just like the feet of Cuckoos, Woodpeckers and Toucans. This type of foot is well-adapted to climbing and clutching or gripping. Some parrots use a foot to hold food and bring it to their beaks, much as a human uses a hand.

Foot shape is important when you choose perches for your bird's cage. A bird that grips the perch, such as a parrot, needs a perch small enough to allow the toes to reach around the perch far enough to grip it firmly. Don't use a perch that is too small either, as it can cause pressure sores.

FROM THE OUTSIDE IN

A bird's feathers, skin, scales, footpads, nails, four sets of cutaneous glands, beak and cere are called the integument. In addition to giving birds an unusually beautiful appearance, the integument offers clues to a bird's health. Feathers and skin can show early signs of emotional stress, malnutrition and illness before the bird begins to exhibit active signs of distress such as sitting on the bottom of the cage or sleeping most of the day.

FEATHERS

A bird has seven distinct types of feathers: contour, semi-plume, down, powder down, hypopenn, filoplume and bristle. Feathers perform many functions including waterproofing, insulating the bird from heat and cold, making flight possible and protecting the skin. They are also used to attract members of the opposite gender in courting rituals.

Feathers help keep a bird's delicate skin in top condition. Areas of the integument not covered by feathers are more likely to become diseased. Such areas include the beak, cere, face, legs and feet.

Feathers grow from follicles in the skin in orderly rows, or tracts. This ensures that the feathers lie smoothly and leave no gaps that would expose the delicate skin. Each feather has a long shaft that narrows from the widest point at the base to the narrowest at the tip. The base of the shaft is called the calamus. The calamus of a fully grown feather is hollow except for thin walls that divide it into narrow cells. These walls are readily apparent when you hold one of your bird's molted feathers up to a window during daylight.

The center part of the shaft, moving from calamus to the opposite end of the feather, is called the rachis. Feather barbs branch from the rachis on both sides. Each feather barb has smaller units, called barbules, branching from both sides. These barbules hook together tightly in a weave, forming the cloth-like surface of the feather. This tight weave helps repel water and refines the bird's aerodynamic shape.

Birds have different types of feathers, each with a distinct function.

An early sign of abnormal feather grooming is when a bird preens excessively or pulls on its feathers, breaking the barbule hooks. This produces a fuzzy, uneven or rough look to the feathers. Malnutrition and other diseases can also produce a rough look to newly forming feathers. Take your bird to an avian veterinarian if its feathers look at all abnormal.

If you pull the barbules apart gently, you can hear a rasping sound. This gives you an indication of how tightly they are fastened together. The interlocking might be compared to Velcro, which also has small hooks. When the feathers become ruffled, the bird corrects their shape by moving each feather through its beak, hooking the barbules and barbs again. The barbs at the base of the calamus are different from those on the rest of the shaft. They do not interlock; they form down feathers where the calamus enters the bird's skin. This adds a protective layer next to the skin.

Feathers are perhaps the most unique physical feature of a bird. Stiff flight feathers on the wings help the bird gain the speed necessary to take off and maintain flight. Softer covert feathers help shape the wing for lift and allow the air to glide softly around the wing, giving the bird lift. There are usually twelve stiff tail feathers that help the bird determine the direction of flight and that act as a braking system when the bird lands.

Blood Feathers and Feather Growth

Mature feathers have no blood supply; they are essentially inanimate. Once grown, they will stay in place for a few months, even a year or more, and then will fall out to allow replacement by a new, strong feather.

Once a feather is molted, a new feather will develop. These new feathers are called pin feathers when they are very small, and blood feathers as they develop. Blood feathers are not a specific type of feather, but rather a young, growing feather that has a blood supply as well as a nerve supply. Feathers grow out enveloped in a sheath and as the feather matures the sheath dries up and is removed by the bird during preening. The resulting feather unfolds into its recognizable shape. During growth a feather can be damaged, causing it to bleed or be broken. If you see blood on your bird, first think of a broken blood feather as the cause. See the section on how to treat bleeding blood feathers later in the book.

Down Feathers

These lightweight, fluffy feathers next to the bird's skin help trap heat and keep the bird warm. Most parrots (Psittaciformes) grow down feathers over their bodies a few days after they hatch. Until then, these helpless chicks depend on the heat of their parents' bodies to keep them warm enough to survive. Others hatch looking like fuzz balls, already covered in down feathers. This first, or juvenile, down is called *natal down.* It is replaced during the first molt by adult down, except in some pigeons and Passerines (a variety of birds that includes Finches and Sparrows). Down color varies from species to species. The arrangement of down feathers on the bird's body also varies by species. If your bird will allow it, gently pull apart the outer feathers on its head or neck or under its wings to look at the down feathers. One sign of abnormal feather grooming is the fuzzy look of feathers on some part of the bird's body. The feathers you see are the down feathers still in place after the bird has sheared off the overlying coverts.

Powder Down Feathers: Powder down feathers break down during normal preening, or grooming. The resulting dust, or powder, covers the bird's body as the bird grooms itself. Powder down helps waterproof the bird's feathers and helps keep them clean. Birds that have powder down feathers include Herons, pigeons, parrots and Bowerbirds. Cockatoos, African Greys and Cockatiels produce the most powder among parrots.

If you pet a Cockatoo, your hand will come away from the bird with a white coating of fine particles that resembles dust. Birds with psittacine beak and feather disease and other serious illnesses often lack the capability to produce powder down. A Cockatoo afflicted with this disease will have a shiny black beak because the beak is not coated with powder down as the bird preens. An inadequate diet can also cause a bird to partially lose the capability to produce the amount of powder necessary to keep its body clean. Many diseases will also indicate an inability to produce powder down.

Contour Feathers

These feathers form the smooth outline of the bird. A bird has more contour feathers than any other type of feather. The number varies, however, depending on the species. A bird uses its contour feathers to help control its body temperature. By raising these feathers, the bird can trap warm air between the contour feathers and the down feathers. To lower its body temperature in hot weather, the bird can pull in its contour feathers, leaving only minimal space between its body, down and contour feathers.

These feathers vary in size and thickness, depending on location. The tiny feathers covering the bird's ears, for example, are fine and thin and allow sound to penetrate easily. It is speculated by some that a bird can also move these feathers to improve reception of sound.

This group of feathers includes the largest and smallest on the bird's body. Contour feathers comprise body feathers and flight feathers including the wing (remiges) and tail (retrices) feathers.

Wing Feathers

Primary and secondary flight feathers grow along the lower edge of the wing. Primary flight feathers are the longest feathers on the wing and are located at the tips. They are asymmetrical, which means they are not perfectly matched on each side. Secondary flight feathers are the shorter wing feathers. They begin at about the midpoint on the edge of the wing next to the primaries and continue on the rear (trailing edge) of the wing to the bird's body. These feathers are held together in a tight bond by small hooks to form what resembles a sheet of feathers, which aids the bird's flight. Think of a fan made of feathers: If there are gaps in the fan, a lot of air gets through. If the feathers weave tightly together, the fan moves a lot of air. On the bird's wing, this gives the bird lift, which helps it take off and fly. The number of flight feathers, secondary and primary, varies from species to species. The outer-most flight feathers are the most important for flight.

Short feathers that lie on top of or cover the bases of other feathers are called coverts. Coverts protect the bases of the feathers they guard. Greater secondary coverts lie on top of the secondary flight feathers. Median secondary coverts lie in a row on top of the series of greater primary and secondary coverts. Lesser secondary coverts are the smaller feathers that lie in the next sequence. The small coverts that form the rows at the leading edge of the wings are called the marginal coverts.

Tail Feathers

The stiff feathers that form the tail are a type of flight feather. When a bird lands, it uses its tail to control the speed of the landing, much like the rudder, elevator and ailerons on an airplane. During flight, the bird can spread its tail to increase the surface area to aid in changing direction. The bird can also manipulate its tail feathers to help gain lift during takeoff. At the base of the tail are covert feathers, overlapping one another in rows. Again, these feathers fasten to one another with hooks to form a connected surface. Each lower feather has small hooks at its end that attach to the feather above.

Young birds often break their tail feathers when playing or just being clumsy. No tail feather is firm enough to support itself; each one relies on the tail feathers beside it for strength. If too many break, there is no support for new feathers when they grow out; the new feathers often break again. The result is a bird that can go for years without a normal tail. Because the bird uses its tail for balance, it will feel clumsy until the tail grows out. To speed this process, an avian veterinarian might elect to pluck all the broken tail feathers, allowing a full tail to grow again. Tail feathers can be plucked easily, and the procedure is not painful for the bird. Other feathers on the body are more firmly attached—especially the flight feathers on the wing—and should not normally be pulled out.

Bristles

These small feathers can be found around the bird's eyes, eyelids, nostrils and beak. It is believed by some that bristles are sensitive to movement. They are formed with a rachis, or shaft, and may have a small number of barbs at the end, adjacent to the skin. In some species, no barbs are present on the rachis.

Filoplumes

There are two types of filoplumes. In the first type, a rachis grows from the nape or breast of some species. In the other type of species, the rachis has a cluster of barbs or barbules at the end. These feathers are located close to the follicle of contour feathers, the exception being retrices or remiges.

Semiplumes

The main shaft of this fluffy insulating feather is longer than its longest barb. Semiplume vanes are downy and light rather than straight and stiff as in flight feathers, for example.

Hypopenn Feathers

Also called the after-feather, this part of a feather grows on the upper part of the calamus, above the downy barbs, on plumaceous and pennacious feathers. Well-developed hypopennae occur in domestic fowl.

The Feather Molt

During this normal occurrence, a bird loses old feathers and new ones grow. Sometimes the new feathers simply replace worn feathers, but in some species, the molt brings in brightly colored feathers used to attract a mate. Wild bird species molt once, twice or three times a year (depending on the species) at set times. The actual pattern of molting is determined by where the bird lives. Birds living in tropical climates have little variation in the weather from season to season, and they molt off and on year-round. Birds in temperate zones molt in the spring and the fall. Most parrots molt continually—they grow new feathers on various parts of their bodies most of the year.

Birds lose their feathers gradually and in an orderly fashion, a small percentage of the total at a time. A healthy bird will not lose all its feathers at once. It is not normal for any bird to look "fuzzy" or have frayed feathers or bald patches during its molt. This means the underlying down feathers are showing through the overlying feathers. Any of these signs means you should take your bird to an avian veterinarian. In most cases, these signs indicate feather-grooming abnormalities; the bird is overpreening, chewing off its feathers or plucking them out.

Owners will notice a few feathers in the bottom of the cage or on the floor of the house as the molt begins. It's important to notice when the bird is molting because, although this is a normal condition, it taxes the bird's body and causes it to be less resistant to disease. Good nutrition, while essential at all times, is especially important during the molt.

THE SKIN

A bird's body skin is relatively thin and lightweight. In some species, it is almost translucent and appears flaky. Although the skin may look pale pink, the color actually comes from the muscles, which you can see through the opaque skin. The part of the bird's skin that lies under feathers is particularly fragile, especially when compared to that of other animals. A bird's skin includes the toenails, beak and cere as well as the scales on its legs and feet.

A bird's skin comprises the epithelium of the epidermis, the connective tissue of the subcutaneous layer and the dermis. The epidermis has a deep layer of living cells and a shallow layer of dead cells. In areas covered with feathers, the epidermis is thinner than in unfeathered areas. In areas uncovered by feathers, including the beak, legs and feet, the epidermis is thicker. This allows it to withstand normal activity.

The skin on the legs and feet of most bird species has compact scales. On the legs, these scales modify gradually from those similar to the foot scales of most birds to the delicate skin found under the feathers. These raised scales are a keratinized epidermis divided by overlays of skin that are less keratinized. These scales become looser on older birds than they are on the younger members of a species. In a wonderful example of adaptation, some birds have feathers on their feet instead of scaled skin. These birds include Owls, Sandgrouse and Ptarmigens.

The skin on a bird's body is attached only loosely to the underlying muscles. On the head, sternum and extremities, the skin is more firmly affixed to the bird's skeletal structure. All areas of the bird's skin are sensitive to touch, heat and cold.

The subcutaneous layer of skin, which is formed by connective tissue, contains fat as well as striated subcutaneous muscles. These are attached to the skeleton and control movement of the skin.

FOOTPADS

Footpads are another part of the integument and are well developed in birds that walk on the ground. They are more developed, for example, in finches, parrots, ostriches and chickens (to name only a few) than in hummingbirds, which rarely climb or walk.

TOENAILS

Bird toenails grow continuously. The sharp tips enable birds to grip surfaces as they climb or walk. In some species, the nails also enable birds to grasp prey and other food. In the middle of each nail is the quick, which contains the blood supply and nerves. Because the dorsal (upper) surface of the nail grows faster than the ventral (lower) plate, the claws curve as they grow.

Wild birds walk on varied surfaces, and this wears down their nails. Birds in homes and aviaries do not wear down their nails as much as wild birds. This may cause the nails to need trimming. Overly long nails put undue pressure on a bird's joints and distort the normal angle of movement of the joints in the feet. Neglected, overly long nails can cause a permanent distortion to the toe as well as arthritis in the joints of the feet.

If you trim your bird's nails yourself, you should take care not to trim into the quick. If you cut the nails too short, they will bleed and put the bird in pain. Whenever you clip nails, have clotting powder or styptic powder available to stop the bleeding. If you let your bird's nails grow too long before taking it to your avian veterinarian, it may be necessary to cut the nails so short that they bleed. The veterinarian will have to do this to protect the bird's toe joints. All nails must be the correct length; if they are too long, your companion could develop arthritis in its joints.

If you do the job yourself, you can use a nail clipper on smaller birds and a larger clipper on larger parrots. Before you try this, take your bird to your avian veterinarian for a demonstration. Make sure that the nails are not trimmed too short; this will make the bird unstable when perching and may cause it to fall and injure itself.

CUTANEOUS GLANDS

Among the most interesting of these organs is the uropygial gland. Most birds, with the exception of Columbiformes (pigeons and doves) and Amazon Parrots, have it. Located on the bird's back at the base of its tail, the uropygial gland secretes oil through multiple orifices, or openings. A cluster of down feathers near the orifices takes up and holds the secreted oil. This tuft of feathers is called the uropygial wick.

When the bird preens, or grooms, its feathers, it rubs its head on this wick and then on other parts of its body. If you watch your bird preen, you can clearly see the wick. This rubbing action spreads the oil over the other feathers to help waterproof them. Other secretions contain the precursors to vitamin D. These precursors activate when exposed to direct sunlight (unfiltered by glass) or ultraviolet light. The bird then ingests them when it preens. The uropygial gland is a good example of several ways in which the bird's body works to maintain health.

Other glands of the integument include the pericloacal glands and those in the bird's ears. Periocloacal glands are located around the vent and secrete mucus. Ear glands release waxy material. Some experts consider the whole epidermis to be a gland in itself, providing immunity as well as structural support.

Birds do not have sweat glands. When a bird overheats, it holds its wings away from its body and pulls its feathers tight and close to its body to avoid trapping warm air. The bird may also pant. It keeps both feet on the perch at this time. Pay close attention to these signs. Overheating can endanger a bird's life. If you notice these symptoms, you may spray the bird with a light mist of warm water. Do not put the bird in front of a fan. Use slow, gentle methods to cool the bird. Try to find out why the bird is overheated and remove the problem. If symptoms persist, see an avian veterinarian.

THE BEAK

The shape of a bird's beak reveals the path the species took as it developed, or evolved, over thousands of years. This specialization reflects the available food and other living conditions in its native habitat. Finches and other seed-eating birds have conical bills, and some parrots have crosswise ridges inside their beaks that help them open and grind hard fruit-stones, seeds and nuts. If you and your bird have established a high level of trust, look closely at your bird's beak for all its special features.

A bird's beak is a versatile tool, comprising of the upper beak and the lower beak. The healthy beak is hard; it is made up of dermis and epidermis, which is thick and hardened. The bird uses its beak to help it climb, eat, pry open seeds and nuts, feed its young, defend itself, attack enemies and preen itself and its flock mates. The bird also uses its beak to reflect its mood; it grinds the beak while it rests and nibbles with it to show

A parrot's curved beak allows it to break open hard seeds and nuts. (Blue and Gold Macaw)

affection. If a bird feels threatened, it might advance on the "enemy" with its beak open to intimidate, sometimes accompanying this action with growls or hisses.

Although it may look like it is made up of dead material, a bird's beak is sensitive. The corium layer, where the beak grows from, is shaped essentially as the beak looks, and the cells grow from the corium layer directly outward in all directions. Think of a cone with active growing cells, continually producing new cells and enlarging the cone. The cone doesn't get any larger, of course, because it is constantly worn down by use. It does not grow from the top down; it always grows outward in all directions.

The beak is comprised of hollow bone with a blood supply and nerves covered by a layer of keratin, the same material that makes up human fingernails. Beaks are sensitive to heat, cold and pressure. The bill-tip organ found on the end of upper beak of many pet bird species serves a sensory function. If you offer your bird something you are eating, the bird may touch the food with just the tip of its beak to sense the texture of the food. It might manipulate that bit of food before it decides to accept or reject it.

Normal beaks are kept healthy when the bird forages for food, builds nests and chews limbs and twigs. In a home environment, a bird needs to chew on toys to keep its beak in shape. If the bird's beak appears to overgrow, this requires the attention of an avian veterinarian for several reasons. The veterinarian must evaluate the cause of the overgrowth and then, only if necessary, trim the beak carefully so the bird can eat properly. Bird owners should never try to diagnose beak problems nor should they ever try to trim a beak. Incorrect trimming could result in serious injury to the bird and a loss of trust. Potential problems associated with malformed beaks include nutritional imbalances, fungal infection and fracture or puncture. Many birds never need their beaks trimmed (Parakeets, Cockatiels, Finches and Canaries, for example). Overgrown beaks and abnormally shaped beaks signify a problem that needs veterinary attention. Some birds that chew aggressively, dig and tear things up in the wild have beaks that grow rapidly. Amazon Parrots and Eclectus Parrots are good examples of this type of birds. Such birds may need regular beak trimming by an avian veterinarian if they do not have hard wooden toys to chew.

The Cere

The cere is located at the top (or base) of the upper beak. In most pet bird species, the nostrils are located in the cere. One exception is the duck (and some other Anseriformes), which has nostrils located lower on the upper beak near the tip. This enables these birds to eat food in the water and breathe at the same time. The cere can serve as another indication of a bird's state of health. If a cere appears misshapen or discolored or if it oozes liquid or shows any other visual change, take the bird to your holistic avian veterinarian for diagnosis and treatment.

THE MUSCULOSKELETAL SYSTEM

The musculoskeletal system of the bird is a marvelous engineering feat. Its many unique adaptations enable most birds to fly.

THE SKELETON

The bones of flying birds, in particular, must be light. They make up only about 10 percent of the total body weight of the bird. In general, birds' bones are light and fragile with thin walls. Many of the bones in a bird's body are hollow; this reduces their weight. Some of the bones have an extension of the air sacs within their center.

The air sacs are part of the bird's respiratory system, sort of an air storage system. Bones that contain air sacs are called pneumatic bones and, depending on the species, may include the femur, humerus, scapula, clavicles, cervical and thoracic vertebrae as well as the pelvis, sternum and connected ribs.

In another adaptation, the bones of female birds can become as much as 20 percent heavier (denser) in preparation for the extra need for calcium during the breeding/egg-laying season. Calcium is pulled from the bones in preparation for eggs. Bones may become fragile at this time, so if you have an egg-laying female, she will need to eat more calcium-rich foods such as carrots.

The bones farther out on the wings and in the legs have modified significantly during natural adaptation so birds can fly instead of walk as mammals do. Many of these bones have become fused. Flightless birds, such as Penguins, Ostriches, and Emus, lack hollow bones.

Bird species have numerous cervical (neck) vertebras, ranging from a low of fourteen in some small species to a high of twenty-five in Swans. In comparison, most mammals, including giraffes, have seven. These cervical vertebras are highly flexible and enable extensive movement of the neck and head. One of the most surprising things for new bird owners is the bird's ability to turn its neck about 180 degrees, a useful capability for wild birds on the lookout for predators or food. This capability also enables the bird to groom the feathers on all parts of its body except its head.

Many of the bones in a bird's body are hollow, reducing overall body weight and making flight easier. (Hyacinth Macaw)

The breastbone, also called the sternum or the keel bone, is necessarily large in many bird species to accommodate the strong muscles needed for flight. In flightless birds, even large Ostriches and Emus, the sternum is flat as opposed to the deep keel shape found in flighted birds, regardless of size.

Bird skulls generally have air spaces, which often makes them weigh less than other animal skulls of the same size. Exceptions include birds that lunge from the air into water for food, such as Pelicans or Kingfishers, birds that use their beaks to hammer into hard surfaces to find food, such as various woodpecker species, and birds that dive from the surface of water into the depths, such as ducks. These birds need strong skulls to withstand the normal physical stressors in their daily lives. The orbital openings (for eyes) and brain cases in birds are large compared to their body size. The bird's eyes must be large enough to capture sufficient light to see deep enough for the proper focal distance, large enough at the back of the eyeball to process light, and big enough to house the optic nerve, which sends information to the brain.

The wing is made up of several specialized bones. The large bone nearest the trunk is the humerus, which rotates away from the body during flight but folds next to the body when the bird is at rest. This bone varies in shape according to the needs of the species. The humerus of diving birds has a different shape than gliding birds, for example, and is longer than in most birds. The humerus of diving birds is comparatively flat.

THE MUSCLES

Another unique feature of birds is that they have both white and red muscles, depending on the principle method of movement (of each species). Red muscle fibers use fat for energy, making them effective for sustained use such as long migratory flights or far-flung searches for food. Birds with red breast, or pectoral, muscles include, but are not restricted to, Hummingbirds, Finches and Parrots.

White muscle fibers, on the other hand, use carbohydrates for energy. Domestic turkeys and chickens seldom fly, if ever. They have white breast, or pectoral, muscles.

INTERNAL ORGANS

THE RESPIRATORY SYSTEM

Birds have unique, highly efficient respiratory systems that include air sacs as well as lungs. The exchange of air for carbon dioxide in the bird's system works differently than in mammals. For one thing, birds breathe in and out far more frequently than mammals. This is necessary because birds need great amounts of oxygen to help fuel their body cells and for flying.

The air a bird breathes enters through the nostrils, the openings located in the cere. It then moves through the bird's sinuses—cavities in the upper beak and skull—and the slit in the roof of the bird's mouth, which is called the choana. The choana acts as a kind of filter and heater for the air before it moves further into the bird's body. From the choana, the warmed, filtered air moves to the throat, called the pharynx, and then into the larynx and trachea. This is the point at which the bronchi, or air passages, split to carry air to the bird's lungs and the air sacs, which vary in number depending on the species.

Unlike human lungs, avian lungs do not expand and contract. Instead, the body wall expands when the air sacs fill, forcing air into and out of the lungs, like the action of a bellows. Birds do not have a diaphragm to separate the chest cavity from the abdomen. Instead, they have a single cavity called the coelom. Oxygen travels to the lung cells from the air sacs and lungs, thus oxygenating the blood.

The efficiency of the bird's respiratory system is a wonderful thing, but it can be the downfall of companion birds. If we, as their caregivers, fail to recognize potential problems, our birds may die. Pesticides, perfume, oven cleaner, spray-on oil, paint fumes, air freshener sprays and other common airborne contaminants can hang in the air. If we fail to remove our birds from a room of our home before we spray these toxins or if we bring our birds back before the contaminants have settled out of the air, we endanger them. The efficient respiratory system of the bird takes in relatively huge amounts of the airborne contaminant in relation to the bird's size, and this can kill the bird.

Nonstick coatings on cooking pans are another source of airborne toxins. Although manufacturers are quick to say that, if used properly, such coatings will not emit toxins, these assurances can lull people into forgetting that levels of toxins in the air that do not cause any noticeable reaction in humans or other mammals can still kill a bird. Of particular danger are items such as nonstick drip pans that fit under stove burners. These routinely reach temperatures far in excess of precautionary guidelines. The best idea is to remove all nonstick items from your household. This will prevent you and any guests from accidentally misusing such items and killing your birds.

If you live with a bird, do not smoke. It's as simple as that. If you or your guests smoke, your bird takes in a huge volume of second-hand smoke. Enforce this simple rule: No smoking inside the house.

THE DIGESTIVE SYSTEM

If you watch a bird eat, you'll see just part of the interesting aspects of its digestive system. When the bird picks up a seed, it does so with its beak. Some bird species hold food with one foot, but many others do not. If the bird is a parrot and has chosen a seed, it will push the seed against the inside of the upper beak with its muscular tongue. Here, ridges that may run from side to side, or horizontally, on the inside of the beak help the bird remove the hull. If the bird is a finch or other softbill, it will use the movement of its sharp lower bill to crush the hull of the seed.

After the seed is hulled, salivary glands in the mouth moisten the seed to prepare it for swallowing. At this time, the choanal opening in the soft palate closes to prevent food from entering the nasal passages. The bird then rolls the seed on its tongue, moving it along toward the esophagus. To prevent the food from being inhaled, the infundibular glottis and the cleft close reflexively. Glands in the esophagus release more moisture, which helps the food move easily along its path toward the stomach.

A bird's esophagus is more thin walled and stretchable than that of other animals. Near the bird's center of gravity. The esophagus expands at the base of the neck to hold the food the bird eats at one meal. This area is called the crop. Although it is readily apparent in featherless chicks, you can feel it in adult birds immediately after they have eaten. After passing through the crop, the food softens and prepares to move at a deliberate pace further along the digestive system to the stomach. In an exception to this, Penguins and Seagulls do not have crops.

A bird's stomach has two parts: the proventriculus and the gizzard. In the proventriculus, also called the glandular stomach, hydrochloric acid and pepsin break down the proteins in the food before it passes along to the gizzard, also called the muscular stomach.

The gizzard of a bird that eats hard-to-digest foods, such as insects and seeds, is well developed. After the food enters gizzard, the muscular walls of this organ crush the food. In birds that mainly eat softer foods, the muscles of the gizzard are poorly developed. The food then moves from the gizzard into the small intestine, where it continues to digest as it is absorbed by the bird's system for use as fuel. From here, the remains of the food move into the large intestine and the rectum. The bird passes the waste material through the cloacal vent. Birds pass waste material, fecal material and urates about once every fifteen to twenty minutes. Removing waste from the body this often helps keep it light, which facilitates flight.

THE URINARY SYSTEM

Waste material, if not removed from the blood, would poison a bird's system. The elimination of some of these toxins is achieved in part by the urinary system. This system also helps govern the delicate balance of electrolytes and water.

In this uncommon arrangement, there is no bladder or holding tank for urine, as in many other animals. With no bladder, there is no need for an urethra. Kidneys produce urine, which is eliminated through the cloaca and vent by way of the ureters. A bladder would simply add unwanted weight to the bird's body as it fills with urine.

Birds produce urine, or urea, which looks like water, and is either clear or lightly colored. They also produce uric acid crystals, which are white-colored solids. Each dropping can contain both urine and uric acid. A dropping can be all feces, all urine or most commonly a mixture of feces in the center with a coating of uric acid around the dropping and a little urine or watery staining around the edges of the dropping.

The Cloaca

Although birds do not have a bladder and usually pass feces out of the intestines frequently, they do have a system to store waste materials when necessary. This is called the cloaca, which is a pouch just inside the body. The cloaca empties through the anus or vent.

The intestines empty into the cloaca by way of the proctodeum. The kidneys empty into the cloaca through the opening called the urodeum. In females, the oviduct passes the egg through the coprodeum during egg laying. The cloaca can act as a storage device just as the bladder and colon can in other animals.

There are many times when a bird does not defecate every few minutes, including at night and when in a nest box. Because birds hold their feces throughout the night, the first dropping in the morning will be large and often watery. As the day progresses, droppings tend to become smaller and dryer.

Normal droppings contain waste from both the intestines and the kidneys. The fecal material should be solid, and the color can range from green to brownish, although foods can alter the normal color to that of whatever the bird ate.

The kidneys produce the watery portion of the droppings, which can be called urine. The kidneys also produce a solid white material that tends to wrap around the feces. (Exceptions include the Budgie and the Parrotlet, whose feces wrap around the urates in a neat circle.) This material is called uric acid or urates. Knowing what is usually in the droppings will help you determine what is normal and what is not.

If a bird eats lots of food that has a high water content—vegetables or fruit, for example—the droppings will have much more urine and will look watery. True diarrhea, however, has a lack of form or solid consistency of the fecal portion of the droppings, not just a lot of water or urine in the droppings.

The Cardiovascular System

Because of the bird's staggering need for efficient delivery of life- and energy-giving oxygen throughout its system, its cardiovascular system is a model of efficiency. The heart is large in relation to the size of the bird's body when compared to mammals, and it beats more rapidly than a mammal's heart. The heart is a four-chambered organ with two atria and two ventricles.

In a unique adaptation, blood flows through the kidneys from the posterior of the bird's body, including the legs, intestinal system and reproductive organs, before it goes to the heart.

The Reproductive Organs

As with the rest of the bird's body, reproductive organs are more streamlined than those of other animals. These organs are internal, making it difficult to determine the gender of some species. If you don't know the gender of your bird because males and females of that species or subspecies look alike, you should have the gender determined using a blood sample. Only then can you evaluate behaviors with any degree of accuracy. Homeopathic remedies and even herbal therapies vary by gender. It is important to know the gender of your bird to help you and your avian veterinarian diagnose any problems. Female reproductive tract disorders are far more common than male reproductive tract problems.

Female birds have two ovaries in the embryonic stage, but the right ovary regresses by the time of birth, leaving only a left ovary and oviduct. When an egg (with a yolk) leaves the female's egg follicle (what we call the egg yolk), it passes through the oviduct. As it moves along, the egg picks up albumin (egg white), two shell membranes and the shell. The process is variable by species and individual, taking from twelve to thirty-six hours. Most commonly, it takes about one day. Another egg might be laid two to three days after each previous egg.

In the male, openings into the cloaca deliver sperm. Many male bird species lack a penis. Exceptions include Ratites, Anseriforms, domestic chickens and turkeys, and Tinamous. Mating birds press cloacas together, which delivers semen from male to female. The male usually stands on the female's back while they copulate.

THE BRAIN AND NERVOUS SYSTEM

A bird's brain is small and well-designed. A reduction in the number of fluid-filled spaces helps decrease the overall weight of the bird. For the size of the animal, however, the bird's brain is large and is roughly proportional to a mammal's brain in relation to its body. When comparing the weight of avian brains in relation to body size, parrots have the largest brain weight and Pigeons, Ostriches and Gallinaceous birds (domestic fowl and Peacocks) have the lowest weight.

As in mammals, when the bird receives sensations or impressions from its eyes, ears, nasal passages, skin and other sites of sensory nerves, these impulses are transmitted from the brain to the spinal cord to relay messages for bodily action or reaction.

THE SENSES

SIGHT

The eyes of most birds work independently of each other, with the exception of raptors. This enables the bird to relay images to its brain from both sides of its head, a necessity in animals that hunt for prey or that may themselves be eaten by others. The bird also is helped by the capability to move its head and neck, manipulating it about 180 degrees.

A bird's senses of sight and hearing are acute; birds see details and discriminate between sounds better than mammals. (Canaries)

A bird has three eyelids: upper lids, lower lids and a nictating membrane that lies closest to the surface of the eyeball. This membrane moves across the eye from side to side to keep the eye moist.

Birds see detail far better than mammals do, another adaptation for finding food and spotting danger. The bird's iris, or pupil, controls the amount of light that enters its eye, just as in humans.

HEARING

On the whole, birds hear very well. Some can discriminate between sounds as much as ten times faster than humans. Some experts believe that birds may not be especially sensitive to higher and lower sounds as well as ultrasonic sounds. The exceptions to this may include Oilbirds and Cave Swiftlets, which live in caves and may need this capability for echolocation.

SMELL

Experts disagree about the capability of birds to smell. Many say this sense is not well-developed in birds except those such as Vultures that rely on it to find food. This theory may have been based on the anatomical fact that the increased visual area of the midbrain seems to occupy space that might otherwise be occupied by the olfactory lobes. In most birds, however, the nasal cavity offsets this; air flows into the cavity and over the olfactory area. Recently, it also has become more generally recognized that Petrels, Albatrosses, Fulmars, Shearwaters and African Honeyguides use smell to locate food or nests.

TASTE

This is another disputed area. Some people believe the bird's sense of taste to be poorly developed, but others note that birds do have taste buds in varying locations, depending on the family group. Parrots, for instance, have taste buds on the roof of their mouth; domestic fowl, pigeons, Swifts, Falconiformes and some songbirds have taste buds at the base of their tongues. For us, the bottom line is that birds obviously have a well-developed sense of taste and have individual preferences based on many factors.

TOUCH

In birds, this sense is similar to that in mammals. Birds feel heat, cold and pain. Nerve receptors in their skin and beaks transmit impulses to the brain and spinal cord as they do in many mammals.

As with all species, what birds like is ultimately related to all their sensory organs. They feel textures, see colors, smell odors and taste items to decide what they like and do not like.

EXERCISE, A NECESSITY

Healthy birds are active for most of every day as they go about normal activities. When we choose a bird as a companion, we need to supply plenty of opportunities for stimulating physical and emotional activity that suits the unique needs of the individual bird. Because we control their environment, it's up to us to provide the opportunity for action.

Most birds should not remain confined in a cage all day, every day. This results in a condition we refer to as cageosis. Cage-bound birds exhibit neurotic impulses such as feather pulling, screaming and endless bouncing or banging their bodies on the sides of the cage. Many people mistake this behavior as happy dancing. You can compare the bird's frustration and resulting mental illness to that of a human who has been kept in solitary confinement with nothing to do for endless periods of time.

An exception to this would be small birds such as Finches that are kept in flocks in large cages or aviaries. These birds carry on their daily activities much as they would in the wild. To keep them happy and healthy give them enough room to fly and interact, plenty of perching spots away from the flight paths, nutritious food and nests or nesting materials.

With other birds, though, you must provide regular activity time outside the cage as well as a rotation of appropriate toys inside the cage. The best way to make sure you give your bird adequate activity time is to create a formal schedule. Every bird should be allowed out of its cage at least twice daily. If your day is busy, let your bird out of its cage for a short time in the morning and then plan the more extensive out-of-cage interaction time in the evening, centered around sharing dinner and evening pastimes.

CLIPPING WINGS: A HAPPY, HEALTHY BIRD CAN FLY

Understanding your bird's wing shape is important when you trim the feathers. A longer set of primary flight feathers allows for a more athletic bird than a shorter wing. Cockatiels have long wings and need a more severe trim than many other birds. An African Grey Parrot or an Amazon Parrot has short wings. If you trim a short wing back as much as you would trim a longer wing, the bird tends to fall too rapidly when it tries to fly, possibly injuring itself. Trim the bird's wing just enough to prevent the bird from gaining altitude, yet allowing it enough lift to let the bird glide down softly to the ground. If your bird falls like a rock after you've trimmed its wings, you'll know the trim was excessive and should be done more conservatively next time.

Experts often recommend clipping all pet birds' wings. Although clipping may be necessary for some birds, we recommend against the practice for most birds. Birds are meant to fly and are most happy and secure when they can. If a bird cannot fly, its cardiovascular system won't work hard enough to remain healthy. They need to fly for fun and

Cockatiels love to fly and may suffer from having their wings clipped.

exercise and to escape from danger. A bird that cannot fly will tend to be more fearful because it knows it is vulnerable.

If you do not clip your bird's wings, you must assume the responsibility of preventing it from escaping to the outdoors, where it will be unable to care for itself. You must also make sure it cannot come to harm by flying into fans, standing water or cooking food. If you have small children, it may not be feasible to have a bird with unclipped wings in the house.

On the other hand, if you clip your bird's wings, you must provide sufficient exercise for its mental and physical health. Out-of-cage climbing ropes, swings and play gyms are a necessity for birds with clipped wings.

Certain birds, such as some Cockatoo and Toucan subspecies, may be difficult to deal with if they remain fully flighted. A Toucan needs an entire room devoted to its needs to be happy and healthy. If you cannot provide for its needs, we recommend against keeping a Toucan as a pet. We have known dedicated bird owners who have designed or built an entire room onto their homes as a safe haven for their birds. Ultimately, you must decide whether to clip your bird's wings based on your bird's personality and needs.

Some birds suffer greatly from clipped wings. Lovebirds, Budgies, Cockatiels and Parrotlets, for instance, take such great joy in flying that they may never quite recover their sense of well-being if their wings are clipped.

Adding perches around a room where you spend time enables you to interact with your bird and gives it plenty of places to land as it flies. For your own peace of mind, remove anything you do not want the bird to destroy. Also take out anything that might hurt your bird such as toxic plants. Make sure all windows and doors are closed properly and are latched so no one can open a door unexpectedly, causing you to lose your bird to the outdoors. If you set a time and stick to it, you and your bird will find this to be the most enjoyable time of the day.

You should offer an array of interesting toys for your bird to chew and play with in its cage. These toys must be appropriate for the size of the bird. Toys too large or too small might injure your bird. We strongly recommend toys made of untreated wood and leather that birds can destroy. Wild birds strip twigs of leaves, tree limbs of bark and nuts of shells. Pet birds need the same opportunities. Such activities occupy their minds and their bodies. After a week, remove the toys from the cage, clean them and replace them with others. This rotation will help keep your bird interested and active. Store the toys you removed to use again in a few weeks on a regular rotation.

Before you introduce new toys to the cage, place them in sight of the cage to let the bird get used to them. Each day, move the toys a bit closer to the cage. When the bird is out of the cage, it may approach the new toys on its own. Never force this action. Some birds will be more wary of new things than others. Knowing your bird will help you keep it healthy and happy.

A LOOK AT A HEALTHY BIRD

When you live with a companion bird, you should spend as much time together as possible during the day. From your first moments of interaction, you can train yourself to really look at your bird and get to know it well. This will enable you to spot problems far earlier than anyone else can. Your veterinarian can help guide you but will not be as familiar as you are with your companion because he or she sees your bird on an irregular basis. Your bird's first line of defense is you.

You can learn to spot early signs of imbalance in your bird, and you can make changes in its environment, both physical and emotional, to help it regain its health. If you live with a bird that does not enjoy hands-on companionship, adapt to its wants. Observe from whatever position it will allow.

Finches and Canaries, for example, may require that you watch them as they interact with each other in their aviary or cage. You can do all but the hands-on examination this way. The main concern is that your bird must be comfortable with the method. A Budgie may allow you to touch it, or it may not. Avoid staring directly at small birds and some large ones. Predators stare at prey, and small birds will feel vulnerable. Frightening the bird will certainly stress it. You can look obliquely at such birds while reading the paper or appearing otherwise occupied.

Set up a pattern. Perhaps you first visit with your bird in the morning before work. If you are not a morning person, perhaps you do your first real visiting in the afternoon when you get home. This will allow you to become accustomed to your companion's appearance and actions at a certain time of the day.

As you greet your bird, look at its feathers. They should shine and should be in good condition with a well-cared-for appearance. Feathers should be in place, a sign that the bird feels well enough to groom itself. The color of the feathers should be similar to others on that part of its body.

A Budgie, for instance, should have uniform stripes on its head and black and colored wavy marks on its wings. The feathers on its abdomen and tail all should look similar to each other. Under the bird's tail, the feathers should be clean and without droppings or staining from droppings on the feathers near the vent. Feathers should not be damaged by chewing or "picking."

A normal bird will molt, losing old feathers to allow new ones to grow in. The number of times the bird molts during a year depends on many factors, including the temperature in your home and the change in the number of daylight hours you experience where you live. Make a mental note of when your bird tends to molt; this will help alert you to an abnormal molt. A bird should never lose all its feathers in a normal molt, nor will it have bald patches. Simply put, all healthy birds have beautiful plumage that is soft and colorful. If your bird falls short of this, it has a problem that needs to be addressed.

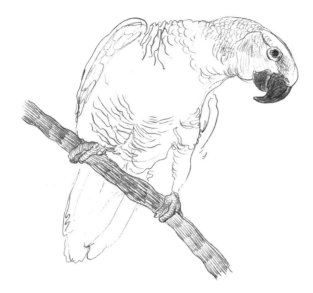

Getting to know your bird's physical attributes, as well as his habits, likes and dislikes, will help you notice signs of ill health and will keep your bird happier and healthier.

Birds that usually have powder down, such as African Greys, Cockatoos and Cockatiels, should have enough on their feathers to leave a coating on your hand after you touch them. Their beaks should also show evidence of powder down. Healthy Cockatoo beaks look gray, because the black beak is covered with white dust. A wet or sick Cockatoo's beak will look black.

Next look at your bird's eyes. They should look clear and bright and should have an intelligent, interested look to them. Pupils (the black part in the center of the eye) should usually be the same size and should not be dilated or constricted all the time. Each pupil can dilate or contract independently from the other. Eyelids should be open except for normal blinking. A bird that looks squinty eyed, with the lids held partially shut, is exhibiting a common sign of illness. The Chinese say that the Shen, or life force, shines through the eyes. Your bird's eyes should radiate health and happiness.

If your bird is comfortable with you stroking its body, check for any abnormal lumps. Look at its feet to make sure the nails are not torn, and the feet and legs should remain free of cuts or other injuries. If you see blood on your bird's feathers, locate the source, which may often be a bleeding blood feather.

Listen to your bird's breathing as it sits calmly on your shoulder, on your hand or on a perch next to you. Never chase and capture your bird to do this because you can stress your bird and lose its trust. In addition, the breath sounds you hear will not be normal. The breath sounds of a calm bird should be quiet; the bird should be breathing through its nostrils with its beak closed. The tail should remain steady as the bird breathes. The nasal passages should remain clear of discharge. Any sneezing should be dry.

A healthy bird holds its wings evenly at its sides. At times, it may rest on its perch with one foot up. If your bird is always resting with one foot up, it may be starting to get sick. Likewise, never resting one foot could mean that a bird is sick. This behavior can be compared to you lying around all day, lacking the energy to get anything done. When they sleep, most birds turn their head toward the back and tuck the beak under the trailing edge of the wing as it rests on the bird's back. This mannerism varies in birds; after a short time, you will know what is normal for your bird.

When your bird yawns, look at the inside of its mouth and at its tongue. Don't force your bird's mouth open. If your bird yawns several times a day, it probably has a sinus infection. It is trying to open up its ears by yawning, just as you do when you feel your ears are plugged (such as when you change altitudes quickly in a plane).

Notice how much your bird eats and drinks each day to establish a norm. Only you and the bird will know what is normal for your bird, and your pet relies on you to interpret the information. Any changes in eating and drinking patterns can be an early warning of problems to come. Eating and drinking less than normal could indicate a problem. Increased thirst is another sign of a problem. What is less commonly understood is that eating too much may be a sign of disease. We often see sick birds whose appetites seemed so robust that their owners never suspected an illness. Sick birds have increased energy needs and they often try to meet those needs by increasing their food consumption.

Get used to your bird's aroma. Each bird has a unique odor, just as people do. As long as the bird remains healthy, it will retain this aroma. Some smell like ginger, pepper, artichokes or other pleasant scents. Any odor from the bird's beak should be pleasant, indicating a normal odor. A bird's droppings should never smell; if they do, there is a problem.

Your bird should maintain a regular schedule and level of activity. Kakarikis and Lovebirds, for example, are active almost all the time and maintain a frenetic activity level. A Finch or Canary may also maintain a high level of activity. An Eclectus Parrot, on the exact opposite of the spectrum, usually exerts very little energy throughout the day.

Many birds wake up with the first light of dawn ready to eat. After they eat, they may play for a while and then nap. They may eat again at midday and then nap again. If the family generally meets for dinner and spends time together in the evening, the bird may adopt this pattern and exert the most energy for play and family interaction in the evening. Your bird will set its own schedule, and you will soon know what that routine is.

A healthy bird usually sits on its perches or on the top of its cage, not at the bottom of the cage. It should rest on one leg with no difficulty, pulling the other one up for a snooze. The resting foot may withdraw into the abdominal feathers in cool weather and remain outside the feathers when the bird feels warm. Some birds, Lovebirds, for example, like to lie around on the bottom of the cage, even burrowing under the cage papers.

As your bird plays inside or outside its cage, make sure its wings work properly. Any odd angles or refusal to fly in a normally active, flighted bird could indicate trouble. Watch as the bird uses all its joints in the legs, feet, wings and neck. Look for any potential stiffness as the bird uses these joints in normal activity.

Look for overall strength and vigor in your bird. Did it have a habit of flying around the room three times but now is tired after only two trips around the room? Did it used to climb vigorously and jump up on its playpen but now seems to labor up the playpen ladder? Such changes in behavior may be early signs of illness.

Each day, look at your bird's droppings. They should be well-formed in a generally round shape (though not perfectly round). Most of the time, the urates form on the outside with the feces on the inside. This can vary. If you know what is normal for your bird, you can easily spot abnormalities. The fecal portion of the dropping should be a dark green to brown. There can be a small amount of water with the dropping (the urine). Droppings that consistently have relatively large amounts of urine (watery droppings) may indicate a problem. There will usually be a white-colored, solid portion of the dropping, the urates. Larger amounts of urates in the droppings could indicate a kidney disease.

Droppings may be other colors if the bird has eaten foods that could influence the hue. Strawberries, beets or red food pellets, for example, could turn the droppings reddish. The droppings should be semisolid without whole pieces of seeds or other foods in them. Droppings should never have an odor; sour, pungent or even sweet-smelling droppings indicate the presence of an intestinal problem.

5

THE BIRD'S EYE VIEW

Your goal as your bird's caretaker is to provide the most stress-free, healthful, enjoyable life possible for your companion. To help you accomplish this, we want you to look at the environment you share with your avian companion from your bird's point of view. After you discover how to do this, you'll begin to see things in a different way. This is an important step in reducing the stress in your bird's life. An environment that suits you or your family well may frighten or upset your bird. An apprehensive, irritated bird may lose its inner harmony or balance. This stress on its system can compromise its body's ability to remain healthy or to heal itself when necessary.

Whether it's a cage or an aviary, your bird's house is its home. Your bird will spend much of its time there.

THE CAGE

When you choose a cage, it's important to put your bird's needs first. Resist any temptation to buy a cage because it matches your decor. Instead, concentrate on such important matters as a size and a shape that suit your bird's physical and emotional needs. Avoid decorative metal pieces, specifically curlicues, because they can entrap your bird's feet or beak.

These artistic touches also catch food, which healthy birds tend to fling with happy abandon. Make sure the bars are close enough together that your bird cannot stick its head through them. A lurking cat could injure your bird, or the bird could get its head or wing caught between the cage bars. Select cages made from stainless steel or powder-coated steel that will be easy for you to keep clean.

CAGE SIZE

Give considerable thought to cage size. Although some birds feel uncomfortable in an excessively large cage, the general rule is "the larger the cage the better." But what size is best? Surprisingly, some smaller birds need the largest cages. A Goffin Cockatoo, although much smaller than a Moluccan Cockatoo, needs a larger cage because its activity level is so much greater than that of the larger bird. The more active the bird, the larger the cage it will need. Many birds are active and love to fly so much that they need a cage as large as a room. This may not be practical, but it highlights the need to bring your companion out of its cage at least twice daily.

Does your bird like to flap its wings? If so, can it flap without hitting other perches or toys? Does it like to fly from end to end? If so, can it fly without running into perches and toys? Perhaps your bird likes to climb. If that's the case, do the sides of the cage have horizontal bars (horizontal bars are easier to climb on than vertical bars) and plenty of ladders to help the bird roam the cage in this way?

PERCHES

In the wild, a bird changes perch diameters as it moves from limb to limb. This keeps the bird from developing sores on the bottom of its feet. Variations in perch diameter mean that birds won't wear away the same spots on their feet all the time. In a cage or aviary, the perch size should also vary from end to end and from perch to perch. If your bird has symmetrically even perches (and wooden dowel perches, for instance), its feet will always have pressure on the same spots. This is similar to a human wearing the same shoes all the time; it could result in sore feet.

Manzanita makes a good natural perch, as does commercially dried and prepared cholla cactus. Other good perches include those made of cotton that are woven tightly so they hold their shape when you bend them. These perches attach to the sides of the cage with plastic caps that screw on the outside of the bars. Half-perches can also work well, offering a bird a spot to sit without as much obstruction as those that stretch across the length or width of a cage.

Avoid perches covered with sandpaper. Although they are intended to wear down nails, they mostly succeed in wearing away the skin on your bird's feet. If you choose colors for the perches, select natural shades such as green and brown to resemble a natural habitat.

From Your Bird's Perspective

As you set up the cage for your bird, you must try to view the new home from your bird's perspective. Think of yourself as the bird sitting in its house. Is it large enough? Exchange places mentally with your bird. Would the cage give you enough room to stretch, fly (for smaller birds) and play with toys? Is there a perch positioned so the bird can easily reach the food and water cups while standing on it? Make sure the other perches are not placed above the food and water cups; you don't want your bird to soil its food and water with droppings.

Is there room for appropriate toys? Are the toys placed so the bird can play with them readily but not positioned in the bird's way when it moves around?

If your bird likes to bathe in the cage, is there room to attach or place the bath? Is the bath large enough for your bird? Are the sides such that the bird can get in and out of the bath? Is it deep enough but not too deep?

Remember, you must think like your bird to decide how to make it happy. To really get into this mode of thinking, watch your bird closely. Note the ways in which it prefers to play, eat and rest. Provide the type of cage and toys your bird will enjoy.

Colors

Some birds are fearful of bright colors or perhaps of specific colors. If you walk into a room in a garish yellow shirt, notice whether your bird becomes fearful. If it does, don't use yellow toys or put yellow furniture near your bird. When you bring new toys into your home, set them near the cage to start. Observe your bird's reaction. Some of the more skittish birds may prefer toys that are the colors of their own feathers. Natural browns and greens are always soothing, safe choices.

Powder coating for cages comes in many hues including shocking pink. If you choose a color, think about it as your bird might. To do this, take into consideration as many factors as possible. With some birds, for example, choosing a cage that's the same color as the bird could be a good choice. Most birds will be happy in blue, green or gray.

Toys

Playing is an important part of a bird's life. Young birds play to learn to deal with their environment and to bond with adults in the flock. Adults play to keep bonds strong within a flock and to practice skills they need to remain alive. Mostly, however, they just play for fun.

It is obvious that no toy can replace the myriad entertainment opportunities available in the wild. Still, we must try to find as many toys as possible for their enjoyment. Continue to supply your companion with as many different toys as you can.

When you select toys, don't forget that your bird will want to chew up the toys. Birds often ignore indestructible toys. Toys made of soft wood that the bird can easily destroy are usually the most entertaining. Watch your bird for clues about the types of toys it enjoys.

Make sure you buy toys that are made for your bird's size. Toys that are too small may break easily in your bird's beak or may entrap unwary beaks or feet. Similarly, toys that are too large could allow your bird to accidentally catch a wing or a leg in the toy, perhaps even breaking the body part.

In addition to destructible toys, some birds like toys they can manipulate or alter and toys they can take apart—and you can put back together. Some of their favorite toys should remain with them at all times, but other toys can be rotated in and out of the cage to provide your bird with some variety. If your bird is apprehensive and does not remember old toys, sit the toys you plan to reintroduce into the cage nearby for a few days before placing them in the cage. This helps your companion to become familiar with them.

Some of the best toys are homemade. The center cardboard rolls from paper towels can be cut up and hooked into a ring for your bird to chew. Cardboard boxes can be turned upside down on top of the cage, enabling your bird to chew up the box and make a temporary nest box. Untreated leather shoelaces can be loosely braided and hung in the cage for your bird to chew or dismantle. Do not make toys from pressure-treated lumber because it is treated with pesticides.

Because your bird needs to spend a lot of time out of the cage, you should also consider a perch or playpen and toys for out-of-cage activities. Does your bird like to climb, swing, chew, perch in a safe spot or fly from perch to perch? Watch how your bird chooses to play and construct a play area to match its needs.

This need not be an expensive proposition. If you want a hanging gym but can't afford a commercial one, you can make one from ladders, cotton rope and plastic rings on which the bird can swing. Some homemade perches and play gyms are extremely innovative. The birds they were made for love them because they were created with the bird's preferences in mind. If your bird likes to fly from one part of the room to another, for example, you could place perches or swings in those areas.

THE HOUSE YOU SHARE

Next you need to look at the larger environment—your home. Where will you create the bird room? This will vary according to available space, but in general, you should find an area that is sunny and cheery, one where your bird can see you when you are at home. This could be a sun room off the kitchen, the family room or a den. Bedrooms and basements are often poor choices because the bird will be isolated. Your bird needs to feel that it lives with you, not isolated from you. It should be an area where you spend much of

In the wild, birds seek homes that offer opportunities for interactivity and security.

your time. From your bird's point of view, the location should offer the opportunity not only for interaction but for security. Look at the room where you will place the bird, imagine the path taken by most people who walk through it, and avoid placing the bird in that path.

Place the cage where your bird can easily see the entrance to the room so your bird will not be startled every time someone enters its space (perhaps an area in a corner near where you commonly sit). This gives the bird two sides of the cage from which it will soon learn it is safe from approach.

It is usually best not to place a cage directly in front of a window. If the window has direct sunlight at any time of the day, your bird might become overheated, and it can be cold at other times of the year. Because it can't leave the cage, the bird will feel exposed in front of the window. It may become afraid of the cats, dogs, people and cars that it can see from the window. It is also best not to place the bird's cage under a skylight because your bird may feel trapped in its cage, unable to fly to safety or to hide from the menace of a circling hawk or crow.

Birds often like to have plants near their cage. Plants calm birds and make them feel safe. Make sure you choose nontoxic plants, and let your bird chew them up. It's great entertainment for them.

HOMEGROWN PREDATORS

Birds are naturally suspicious. With this in mind, look around your home for predators. Remember, you are looking at this from your bird's point of view. Cats, dogs, mice, hamsters, gerbils and larger or more aggressive birds all represent potential dangers in your bird's mind. Children and adults who may tease or mistreat your bird are other dangers you should consider.

Once you begin attempting to see things as your bird might, you will find it increasingly easy. If your bird seems frightened by a location, a situation, a person or an animal, it's up to you to take appropriate long-lasting action.

PREVENTING PHYSICAL PROBLEMS

As you walk around your home, begin to view it with an eye to your bird's safety. Keep toilet lids shut; you don't want your bird flying into the toilet and drowning. Keep electrical cords away from places where your bird plays. Keep windows and doors closed so your bird doesn't fly away. Never, under any circumstances, spray insecticides, air fresheners or perfumes near your bird.

Birds are naturally curious. Pet birds can become so relaxed about their surroundings that they feel quite comfortable chewing on and testing anything lying about. Dangerous items include jewelry, stained-glass windows and lamps, drapery weights and old paint, any of which could contain lead. Cigarettes, alcohol and toxic plants will also physically harm your bird.

Safe Plants

Putting plants around your bird's cage may help it feel more secure, but you can count on your bird to chew on the plants. This means you must make sure that these and all other plants to which your bird has access are nontoxic. The list included here is by no means complete. One way to research plants is to use books that concentrate on plants safe or nontoxic for small children. These books should be available at your local garden store or your library.

Safe plants include: *Bromeliads, Scheffleras, African violets, roses, ferns (asparagus, Boston, bird's nest, maidenhair, ribbon, staghorn, and squirrel's foot), cacti (Thanksgiving, Christmas, and Easter), hibiscus, mango trees, Dracaena, any ficus, palms (bottle, ponytail, can, golden feather, Madagascar, European fan, sentry and pygmy date), Aloe, burro's tail, Coleus, gardenias, grape ivy, hens and chicks, jade plants, Kalanchoe, Pepperomia and yucca.*

Avoid feeding artificial fertilizers or systemic pesticides to plants in your home because they may be ingested by your bird and could cause illness or death.

Toxic plants that should be kept far from your bird's reach include Amaryllis, bird of paradise, Calla lily, daffodil, Dieffenbachia, English ivy, foxglove, holly, juniper, lily of the valley, mistletoe, oleander, Philodendron, Rhododendron, rhubarb, sweet pea and wisteria. (This is just a partial list.)

THE EMOTIONAL ENVIRONMENT

It is often easier to sort out physical dangers in your home than to recognize and change situations that can damage a bird emotionally. A wild bird has many options that a companion bird has lost. Foremost of these is that, when a wild bird feels afraid, it can fly away. If your bird believes it is in danger, it can't leave. You must provide an environment in which your bird feels safe.

A wild bird can forage for just the right foods that it needs each day. You bird must eat what you provide; try to be consistent with meal times and conscientious about feeding your companion a nutritious diet.

Birds feel safest when they know what is going to happen around them. If birds could select a motto for us all to live by, it might be "Routine is good." Remember, your bird is dependent on you. You must also realize that your bird is an individual with desires and needs of its own. Instead of you forcing your bird to act the way you want it to behave, you must try to provide as much freedom as possible. Perhaps there is no statement more important than this: The ability to act, whether it is fruitful immediately or not, can make the difference between mental health and mental illness.

The inability to act and use the natural chemicals that flood the bird's body can be destructive and can disturb the natural balance in its body. Provide a safe environment and give the bird some control over its daily activities.

Birds are highly emotional animals. Once they bond to you, your birds will be strongly affected by anything that upsets you. Arguing with friends or relatives in front of or in hearing range of your bird is not a good idea. If you or any of your friends or relatives use loud voices, throw things or make sudden violent moves during disagreements, consider the feelings of your bird. It has no real idea of the outcome of the battle, and it knows for sure that you are upset. Consider keeping these battles out of the home or reducing the level of intensity. This might help the human participants, too.

Cageosis is a condition commonly seen in birds that rarely, if ever, leave their cages. This is cruel treatment and can result in mental illness in the bird. Imagine yourself confined to a room with no chance of leaving, no interaction and no stimulation.

Wild birds are busy from shortly after they wake up at sunrise until it's time to go to sleep. They hunt for food, fight off or hide from prey, protect each other, play together and take care of their young. To survive, birds have amazing intelligence and physical agility. Companion birds have the same makeup and the same instincts. When permanently confined to cages, however, they either waste slowly away in deep depression or bounce, scream and mutilate themselves. This is considered to be mental illness, and it is preventable.

Our birds have no food-finding chores; we provide all their food. In most cases, they don't have to hide from or fight off predators; we give them a safe environment. They cannot play and interact with the members of an avian flock; they live among humans. This could be a bleak picture and, for some birds, it is. As their companions and guardians, we can help prevent this. Give them consistent, loving companionship and let them set many of the boundaries of your relationship with them. Make them intimate members of your family. Even better, view your relationship with your bird as if you are joining their flock—you must learn to interact with them.

6
NUTRITION

Any discussion of nutrition should start by explaining what we don't know about the nutritional needs of birds. There is less research about bird nutrition than any other group of animals and little significant nutritional research about any birds other than poultry. All the guidelines we use are based on research done on poultry and nonavian species of animals.

Complicating the study of avian nutrition are the sheer numbers and differences among species as well as the varied ecosystems in which the different birds live. Even keeping within relatively similar species, the psittacines (parrots) living in Australia eat far different diets than the birds in Africa or South America. Even similar species living in the same country often eat diets far different than their related species. It has been documented that Amazon Parrots and Macaws living in the same Amazon River ecosystem have dissimilar diets.

When discussing avian nutrition, we can make only generalized statements because each species is so different from any other species. Based on information available at this time, you should feed your birds a large variety of foods and should avoid foods that are high in fat, sugars, salts, chemicals or preservatives. Birds that are primarily seed and grain eaters, such as parrots, should be fed predominately seeds and grains. By adding a variety of fruits, vegetables and some meat to their diet, however, you are more likely to cover all the nutritional bases.

One thing is clear: The outdated method of feeding seeds to birds and then trying to "balance" their diet by adding vitamins and a calcium supplement should be abandoned. Vitamin supplements are only of marginal benefit because they do not supply the coenzymes, cofactors, enzymes, micronutrients and trace minerals found in whole foods.

The key to good health, in general, is in eating fresh, minimally processed foods in variety and not eating excessive amounts of any food group. A bird's body thrives on whole, fresh foods. A current trend recommends feeding birds a formulated commercial diet. We cannot recommend this method because we do not believe it offers optimum nutrition to birds. People should not restrict their birds' diet to only highly processed foods. It would be absurd if someone told us that the best diet for us is a pelleted diet—the same pellet for every meal, day in and day out. We know much more about what the human body needs nutritionally, and we are told continually that we must eat a variety of different fresh foods daily. Why would birds be any different? Although feeding your bird a certified, organic, pelleted food can be a good addition to its diet, using the pellet as the entire diet is inadequate and unappealing for birds.

Unfortunately, when pellets were first introduced in the early to mid-1980s, too many people took some manufacturers' claims as truth. They assumed that the pellets alone were a complete diet. Based on inflated claims of nutritional soundness, and perhaps even more on the ease with which they could feed their birds, many people began feeding their avian companions only pellets. The results were often disastrous. Although it is a little more time consuming, we believe that people who feed birds formulated commercial diets should also include fresh, unprocessed foods in their companions' diets.

It's How You Do It

It would be nice to just place a food bowl overflowing with fresh food in a cage and expect the bird to eat a little of everything in the bowl. More likely it will eat a few of its favorite things and leave the rest on the cage floor or in the bowl. In their natural habitat, parrots consume a variety of foods including seeds, nuts, grains, sprouts, leaves, insects and fruits. Some eat meat in the form of mice, small birds and carcasses. Typically, all birds subsist entirely on one type of food when it is plentiful. When birds eat, they are vulnerable to predators. They want to eat as much as they can as fast as they can and then return to the safety of their tree. Seeds are easy to eat rapidly, and when a bird has free access to all the seeds it wants, it consumes large amounts of seed. Instinct tells them to do this, and they follow through.

As a result, birds naturally become "addicted" to their favorite foods if they are allowed free access to the food items they like the most. They don't really become addicted but accustomed to what they eat, the same as humans. Because birds are genetically programmed to fill their crop rapidly—and they're suspicious by nature when new foods are offered—if left to choose, they will tend to eat only the most tasty, familiar treats offered.

Birds will tend to eat only the most tasty, familiar treats offered if they can choose for themselves.

To learn to correct a bird's eating habits, it is important to refer to the behavior of wild birds. When their favorite food source is no longer available, wild birds become hungry. This triggers the foraging instinct and pushes them to seek out new food sources.

It works the same way with companion birds. When you provide your bird with free access to seeds, the bird loses its foraging instinct. Your bird will then choose to subsist entirely on seeds. Offering new foods often fails to broaden the diet unless you severely limit the food items your bird relishes most. The best method to alter the diet of the "seed addict" is to limit the total amount of all the different food items you provide. The eternally full food cup creates picky eaters that consume only a limited variety of foods.

Developing a Feeding Schedule

Feed your bird on a twice-daily schedule. This technique approximates normal food gathering in the wild and induces birds to sample new food items. Providing access to food throughout the day inhibits the foraging instinct and may cause your bird to become obese.

For many people, the best routine is to feed seeds and other dry food items such as pellets, nuts and whole grains in the morning. Most people are not at home during the day and are not able to remove the "wet foods" from the cage after two to three hours when spoilage could occur.

Feed your bird such a small amount of its favorite foods that it will finish them in the first ten to fifteen minutes. The bird can then eat the foods it likes less throughout the morning (the pellets). Either remove the food cups by midday or place such a small amount in the food cup in the morning that your bird will have emptied the cup by that time. The bird should have no food available for several hours leading up to the second meal of the day.

Having no food available for several hours accomplishes at least three things. First, it allows the bird's body to process the food and detoxify itself. Only through fasting between meals can the body process food correctly and excrete toxic by-products. The second thing this system accomplishes is that it provides time for the bird to become hungry for its afternoon/evening meal. Finally, feeding only small portions of the various dry food items keeps the bird from self-selecting only its favorite foods.

The evening is the best time to feed your bird foods that could spoil if left in the cage too long. You may be around throughout the evening to remove the food after three hours in the cage. Most people tend to prepare meals in the evening, so it is easier to include in your bird's food cup the healthy foods you eat at the evening meal. This is when you can offer vegetables, fruits, cheeses, meats, beans and eggs. Remember, any food that can spoil should never be left in the cage longer than three hours.

WHAT TO FEED?

This simple rule will go a long way for you: Never feed anything to your bird that you couldn't eat yourself, but remember, even though you may not like broccoli, your bird may love it! But make sure all fresh foods you feed your bird are clean; birds are at least as sensitive as we are to food poisoning, chemicals and toxins. Choose only fresh fruit and vegetables at their peak. Either type of food should be firm and have good color without excessive bruising. Fruits and vegetables should be carefully cleaned to remove wax and pesticides before storing or feeding. Remove the wax from the fruit by soaking it in warm water and a little biodegradable soap. Scrub off the wax with a clean plastic scrubber. Unless you remove the wax from the fruit, you can't wash off the pesticides trapped beneath the wax.

Rinse the fruits and vegetables well in cool water. Let them dry thoroughly on clean paper towels before storing them in the refrigerator's vegetable crisper.

HOME COOKING FOR BIRDS

The dry-food diet fed in the morning can include some seeds, nuts, grains and a few pellets of a formulated diet. In the evening, feed your bird soft foods. Some of the best food items are highlighted below in darker print. If there are no emphasized items in a category, consider them to be all of equal merit.

We also have included several recipes you can select from as well as providing fresh fruits and vegetables.

Fruits: *Fruits can make up 10 percent of the diet on a daily basis.*

Good fruits to select from:	Other fruits to consider:
Cantaloupe	Oranges
Apricots	Mangoes
Apples	Raisins or grapes
Bananas	Pears
Papayas	

Disinfectants, Bug Sprays and Mite Protectors, Oh My!

Most of us grew up with certain cleaning routines that we bring to our own lives as adults. Unfortunately, some of the most basic routines can be extremely harmful to our companion birds such as the habitual use of disinfectants and insecticides.

Routine use of disinfectants to clean your bird's cage, cups and toys is both unnecessary and potentially harmful for your bird, yourself and the environment. It is best to simply keep the cage clean: Change water bowls two or three times daily and keep the perches and bars clean using just a little soap and water.

It is impossible to really disinfect a bird's cage. Toys can't be disinfected because the disinfectants won't work on porous material (perches, wooden toys, ropes). Numerous scientific studies have shown that soap and water remove the vast majority of potential problems and that disinfecting helps only a little.

In hospitals, for example, it has been shown that simply cleaning a countertop with soap and water removes roughly 95 percent of the bacteria, viruses and fungi. Adding a disinfectant removes only an additional 2 to 3 percent. The same studies have shown that the countertop will return to the previous level of bacterial contamination within as little as four hours whether it was cleaned with soap and water or disinfectant. In other words, it is impossible to sterilize your bird's cage.

Most of the bacteria in your bird's environment came from your bird's feet and beak or the food it ate. Your bird is already resistant to infection from these bacteria. The few new germs it is exposed to will, in almost all cases, be a healthy stimulant to its immune system and provide immunity against future germs.

Disinfectants are poisons. Look on the label; it will tell you that the product is harmful if taken internally. Your bird does not wear shoes, and if you apply a disinfectant to the perch or bars, your bird will absorb small amounts of the toxic disinfectant through its feet, tongue and mouth when climbing around. It will also inhale them, which can lead to disease over time. Constant exposure through the skin and by breathing the vapors is also harmful for you.

Recent studies show that routine use of disinfectants creates "super bacteria" that are more deadly than ever. This is similar to the overuse of antibiotics causing bacteria that are resistant to all known antibiotics.

Routine use of disinfectants won't remove any more germs than simple cleaning does. Disinfectants are toxic to various organs in the body and are known carcinogens. Finally, although they almost never prevent infections, they are likely to make sure any infection your bird gets is more deadly than if your avian companion had not been exposed to disinfectants.

Similarly, insecticides can harm or kill your bird. If you live in an area where routine spraying by professionals is considered necessary, caution must become your watchword. Many professional sprays are so toxic that the fine print on contracts cautions against allowing any children or pets to have contact for as long as a week after the spray. Such sprays can kill your bird in several ways. If your companion is in the room when the insecticide is applied, the bird may breathe the toxic chemicals. The fumes from the chemicals linger in the air for some time and continue to have the potential to kill your bird. If you must use an insecticide, ask the company representative to spray only outside.

You may occasionally see recommendations to use insecticide in your bird's cage or nest box to kill pests. Never use any insecticide in or around your bird's cage. Inside each container of mite protector, a commonly sold product, is an insecticide that is as toxic as any other bug spray. Placing one of these items in a bird's cage is adding unnecessary toxicity; pet birds rarely have mites because they are not generally exposed to them. If you suspect that your bird has mites, take it immediately to an avian veterinarian for proper diagnosis.

For your bird's health and your own, do not use disinfectants, insecticides or mite protectors.

Vegetables: *Fresh steamed or lightly cooked vegetables can make up 15 to 20 percent of a bird's daily diet.*

Good vegetables include:	Poor-quality vegetables to avoid:
Sweet potatoes	Iceberg lettuce
Broccoli	Celery
Pumpkins	Potatoes
Beets	Corn
Dark-green, leafy vegetables	
Endive	
Kale	
Parsley	
Carrots	
Squash (summer and winter)	
Capsicum peppers (chili peppers, bell peppers)	

Grains: *Seeds and grains should make up the majority of most birds' diets. For psittacines (parrot-type birds), 60 percent of their diet should be seeds and grains. Seeds should make up approximately 75 percent of a canary or finch diet. Some people prefer safflower seeds over sunflower seeds because of the common myth that sunflower seeds contain a compound called papaverine, which is purportedly addictive. Neither safflower nor sunflower seeds contain papaverine, and either is appropriate. We tend to like sunflower seeds because of the relatively balanced protein content and because safflower seeds have a bitter taste.*

It is best to buy the striped or white sunflower seeds and not the black ones. Black sunflower seeds contain too much oil and often have more contaminates. They are not considered nutritious enough for human consumption; therefore, they are not good enough for your bird.

Offer a good-quality mixture to your bird; it will soon become evident which seeds the bird will eat. Some birds eat safflower seeds; others prefer sunflower seeds. Still others favor millet and other small seeds found in a mix.

High-fat seeds: *Feed these seeds sparingly or the total fat content of your bird's diet will be too high; too much of the bird's total daily calories will be taken up by these seeds. High-fat seeds and legumes commonly found in commercial mixes include peanuts, thistle, safflower, sunflower, pumpkin, hemp and flax. The "average" 500-gram parrot, such as an African Grey, an Amazon Parrot, an Eclectus or a Cockatoo, should be fed no more than ten to fifteen high-fat seeds daily.*

- Sunflower: eight to ten per day for most parrots

- Safflower: fifteen per day for most parrots

- Peanuts: We do not recommend them. If you decide to feed them to your bird anyway, offer only one or two.

Non-oily seeds and grains: *These should make up the majority of most birds' diets. Millet, canary seed, buckwheat, rye, wheat, oats, milo, barley, corn and rice are all good grains. Rolled grains such as oatmeal are fine, too. Rice should be cooked, but the others can be fed fresh or cooked into breads. At least some of the grains should be fed fresh daily and not cooked or baked. Whole grains can also be soaked to soften them.*

It's important to use fresh seed because it contains the most nutrients. You can find out whether the seed is fresh by trying to sprout it. Cut a piece of a new sponge into a small square. Put it in a small bowl of water until it has absorbed the liquid. Place the wet sponge on a flat container in the sun and sprinkle some seeds on the top, working them into the holes of the sponge. If you keep the sponge damp, fresh seeds will sprout. Do not feed these to your bird because you have not controlled the possible growth of bacteria or mold.

Germinating Seeds: *Sprouted seeds are a valuable addition to any bird's diet. Sprouting them is easy but must be done carefully. The best candidates are millet, wheat, oat and sunflower seeds. Broccoli and other vegetable seeds can also be sprouted and are excellent additions to the diet. For one or two birds, place a tablespoon of seeds in a bowl. Cover the seeds with tepid water. Cover the bowl and leave them for about twelve hours if your house is warm or twenty-four hours if your house is cold. During this stage, rinse the emerging sprouts twice daily in dry climates.*

At the end of the twelve- or twenty-four-hour period, rinse the seeds well. Look carefully for any that ooze a liquid thicker than water or that appear to have fungi or mold growing on them and remove them. Dry the sprouted seeds on a fresh, white paper towel and feed them to your birds. Throw away any they do not eat in about an hour to avoid the possibility of digestive upsets due to spoiled food. After the seeds finish sprouting, you can keep them refrigerated for up to three days, but throw out any remaining sprouts after that.

OTHER RECOMMENDATIONS

Nuts: *Nuts are seeds, but we will discuss them briefly as a separate entity. Nuts are high in oils. Some of the more appropriate nuts to feed your bird include almonds (high in calcium), macadamia nuts and walnuts. Feed no more than one or two nuts daily per bird.*

Peanuts: *Peanuts contain aflatoxins, which are fungal toxins found with all seeds, grains and nuts. Aflatoxins are hepatotoxic. This means they kill liver cells. The levels of aflatoxin in most seeds are insignificant, but higher levels can be found in peanuts than in other nuts and grains.*

Legumes: *Legumes provide an excellent source of proteins and are relatively low in fat. This makes them a good addition to the diet for many birds. Cook dried legumes, although fresh legumes are valuable additions to the diet as well. Legumes can make up 25 percent of the diet. Legumes to include are peas, navy beans, kidney beans, mung beans and soy beans.*

Animal proteins: *Meats are not required in the diet of most birds. Some of the obvious exceptions are birds of prey, toucans and mynahs, and fish-eating birds such as pelicans. Meats can be fed in small amounts to most birds, however, and some birds, such as African Grey Parrots, Amazons and Cockatoos, seem to relish them in the diet. It's best not to feed meats daily. Perhaps up to 5 percent of the diet every few days.*

Eggs are commonly fed to companion birds. (Canaries eat commercially made egg food, for example.) The egg yolk has often been called the perfect source of protein because it contains all the essential amino acids. Eggs can be fed in small amounts, but they are not needed on a daily basis.

Handle all animal products carefully, cook them thoroughly and refrigerate them properly to prevent bacterial infections. Wash your hands after handling them so you don't recontaminate cooked foods.

Calcium Sources: *Traditionally, most birds have been given calcium sources such as cuttlebone fish, oyster shell and mineral blocks. We do not recommend this approach because it is highly unnatural for birds to eat calcium in these forms, and it is an inefficient method of calcium supplementation. In addition, cuttlebone, the skeleton of the Cuttlefish, may be contaminated because many habitats in which this fish lives are polluted.*

Other people recommend that dairy products, yogurt and cheeses be fed to improve calcium intake. Although we have no problem with feeding birds limited amounts of dairy products, we believe that the best source for calcium (and most other minerals) is organically grown vegetables. It may come as a surprise to some, but there is more calcium in one carrot than in a quart of milk.

Calcium absorption is difficult at best. Some forms of calcium pass through the gastrointestinal tract with almost no absorption. Cuttlebone, mineral blocks and oyster shells

Calcium Sources

Calcium is the most plentiful mineral in the body. Breeding hens and hens that lay eggs without breeding need more calcium than other birds because egg formation requires calcium. For this reason, we are including the following list of foods that are highest in calcium.

Almonds	Figs
Apricots	Hazelnuts
Beans	Kale
Bran	Lemons
Broccoli	Limes
Cabbage	Oranges
Carrots	Parsnips
Eggs	Tofu
Endive	Watercress

are inorganic calcium. Organically bound calcium is found in foods. It is well established that organically bound calcium is far more readily absorbed into the body than inorganic calcium. To maximize calcium uptake and use, feed your birds whole foods.

Water: *Fresh, clean water should be available at all times. Water bowls should be changed at least twice daily to maintain cleanliness. People often ask if public water supplies are safe for birds. This is a difficult question to answer, in large part due to the extreme variation between different water supplies.*

Some people are concerned with the potential for Giardia infections from public water supplies. Giardia is an intestinal parasite. There is little chance any bird can develop Giardia infections from this source because Giardia is rarely found in drinking water. When Giardia is in water, it most often originated from mammals; it may infect only other mammals, not birds.

Water Filters

We recommend that birds be given bottled water or water from a good home-treatment system. Home-treatment systems can be confusing, though. Here is a brief description of several types.

The type of treatment system to acquire depends on what problems your water supply has; therefore, it is best to have your water tested. Alternatively, public water departments should have an analysis on file, and you can request a copy of it.

In general, the types of contaminants to be concerned about include:

- Bacteria, Giardia/protozoa, cryptosporidium
- Inorganic chemicals (such as nitrates)
- Organic chemicals (such as pesticides, industrial chemicals)
- Chlorine and fluorine
- Minerals (hard water)
- Sediment, particulate matter

Reverse osmosis *filtration generally removes inorganic contaminants, such as nitrates.*

Mechanical filtration *removes sediment and microbes, such as Giardia, bacteria and cryptosporidium.*

Activated charcoal *is best for removing organic materials such as pesticides, herbicides and the trihalomethanes formed by chlorinating water. Some systems combine all of these types of treatment and would be the right choice if your water supply has problems in all three areas.*

Water distillers *are available as well, but we do not recommend them. They tend to remove healthy minerals and may not remove volatile organic compounds (pesticides) and microbes, such as Giardia cysts.*

The last type of water treatment is a **water softener.** *This is good at removing minerals, including lead and iron, but it does nothing for bacterial contaminants, Giardia cysts, nitrates or pesticides. If the only problem you have is hard water, these devices are effective.*

Of more concern are the levels of various chemicals in the public water supply. Some supplies are remarkably high in nitrates, for example. Others may contain unacceptable levels of lead, pesticides, petrochemicals and various other toxins. In all, more than 2,100 toxic chemicals have been found in our water supplies.

Some municipalities have notably pristine water; however, even these may contain high levels of chlorine. Chlorine levels within the same water district often vary widely, and they may vary in one location throughout the day as well. Chlorine has been shown to increase certain types of cancer (such as bladder cancer) in people who drink chlorinated water all their lives. Chlorine can combine with different organic chemicals to make carcinogens and other toxic substances. Public health officials believe that the benefits (protection from bacterial infections in the water) far outweigh the problems. Holistically minded medical practitioners are more concerned, and most recommend that we should drink chlorine-free water.

Grit: *Traditionally, birds have been fed grit or sand to help their gizzards grind food. Recently, many aviculturists have stopped feeding grit to their birds. Some believe birds that hull their seeds do not need grit, and those that do not hull their seeds (Pigeons, Doves) need grit to grind up the seed hull. This view is still controversial; most birds in the wild have sand or grit in their gizzards. The presence of the grit surely aids in grinding and digesting food.*

Some sand in a bird's gizzard will grind and digest food more efficiently. Although it is true that many birds seem to digest food adequately without the presence of grit in the gizzard, many birds have markedly improved their digestion and health after the addition of grit to their diets.

It is not recommended that cups of grit be made available to birds. Some birds given free access to cups of grit eat too much of it and end up with so much sand or grit in their gizzards that there's no room for seeds. Others seem to have impaired digestion with excessive grit in the digestive tract. Those of you who want to provide adequate grit can place a few pieces in the seed cup every couple weeks. Again, birds should not have grit available all the time.

Finally, some people feed oyster shell as the source of grit. Oyster shell is not grit; it dissolves in stomach acid soon after consumption. Further, some sources for oyster shell are contaminated with heavy metals, pesticides and petrochemicals.

Formulated Diets: *Formulated diets (pelleted diets) are now commonly available. Formulated diets can help provide a more balanced diet than seed diets, and they are preferable to feeding just seeds. Formulated diets are not preferable to feeding your bird high-quality fresh food, however. Some bird caretakers seem to be incapable of feeding fresh foods in variety and enforcing the consumption of all the food groups. They should serve their birds a formulated food as the basic food source and supplement extensively with fresh foods.*

To Preserve or Not to Preserve

In any discussion about prepared foods, we have to consider the use of preservatives. The preservatives in current use are ethoxyquin, BHT and BHA. These products are designed to protect fats from oxidation (becoming rancid). Rancid fats produce carcinogens.

Traditional pet-food manufacturers have long held that the improved shelf life of preserved food is worth the risk of adding preservatives. Chemical antioxidants (preservatives) are assumed by them to be safer than the carcinogenic compounds that develop when fats become rancid. This may be true, but we want to point out that there are a number of potentially detrimental effects other than the carcinogenic potential of the preservative versus rancid by-products.

There are several other ways to preserve fats. They can be processed in a way that minimizes the risk of oxidation. They can be stored in containers that protect the product from the sun. We can buy smaller quantities at a time and use them sooner. The manufacturer can add enough vitamin E to retard spoilage.

For years, holistic doctors, veterinarians, health-care practitioners and nutritionists have opposed chemical preservatives. Now the public wants preservative-free food for their pets. After years of claiming that there are no negative effects from the use of ethoxyquin, the manufacturer recently (and quietly) agreed with the FDA to cut in half the amount that the company formerly considered safe to use for pets.

Some of the largest manufacturers of pet foods, companies that once claimed it was not possible to produce diets without preservatives, are now converting their entire line of animal feeds to preservative-free diets. In other words, it was never impossible to produce safe, high-quality products without the use of preservatives. It was always an issue of profit. They could make a bit more profit than if they used vitamin E to preserve the diet.

The public has determined that the risks of consuming relatively large amounts of preservatives now outweigh the potential benefits, so manufacturers are complying with public demand and providing preservative-free diets that are safe and will not spoil.

Everyone should learn to read labels on pet food. Consider using products that contain no preservatives, food colorings, synthetic vitamins and other chemicals (their names often begin with the prefix "dl-"), processed sugars (glucose, dextrose and sucrose) and by-products. The term "by-product" is used to describe whatever is left after everything that can be used for people is removed. Harder to determine, but just as important, is the length of the ingredient list; the longer the roster, the poorer the quality of food the manufacturer starts with. They are being forced to add various compounds to make the diet nutritionally complete. A manufacturer can achieve the same results by starting with high-quality food. We also need to remember that a good diet is not cheap, so be prepared to pay much more for a quality product.

We believe in feeding organically grown foods whenever possible. At this time, there is only one certified organically grown formulated diet on the market, the Harrison Bird Diet. We find this diet to be a well-conceived pellet, and it is often accepted well by birds.

A formulated diet could be used as a part of the total diet—including it at perhaps 25 to 50 percent of the diet—with the remaining foods comprising all of the previously mentioned food items.

Nutritional Supplements: *The question of what supplements are necessary is complex and varies by the species and the individual bird. When a bird eats a high-quality, organically grown diet with plentiful fresh foods, it is difficult to make a case for feeding a nutritional supplement to every* *bird. Birds with diseases, genetically weakened birds and birds under stress all might have an increased need for nutritional supplementation. Unfortunately, no single supplement fits all needs.*

Many manufacturers of supplements claim to benefit every bird. These claims often leave the potential buyer with the impression that a specific product can cure all of a bird's ills. Most come with glowing testimonials to their effectiveness. Many are multilevel marketed. We are not opposed to ethical marketing, but multilevel products often seem to be the greatest offenders of the "miracle cure" sales pitches. In addition, because testimonials are mostly exaggerated, you should require any person selling you a product to provide specific evidence of his or her competence. There are no miracle products or cures, and none work for all birds. If you read an ad for a supplement that claims to be what all birds need for optimum health, you can be assured that the marketing of that product is a hoax.

When you supplement a bird's diet with various nutrients, it is essential that you use as many whole foods as possible. This is in opposition to the common practice of providing vitamin and mineral supplements made from synthetically processed vitamins and amino acids.

You would be surprised at the minimal amount of original research used to determine essential vitamins. In fact, the body and its nutritional needs are so complex that literally hundreds of essential nutrients are needed to maintain health in all situations.

Let's look at vitamin C, for example. Some people believe that vitamin C is ascorbic acid, the chemical found in all traditional supplements. We do not believe that this is the only chemical in vitamin C. Scurvy is a disease caused by a lack of vitamin C. It has long been known, however, that all symptoms of scurvy cannot be removed by simply adding ascorbic acid to the diet. The minimum daily recommendation (recommended daily allowance, or RDA) for ascorbic acid is 60 milligrams. Yet many healthy people from northern countries, such as Alaskan natives, never take in an amount even close to this minimum requirement.

How is this possible? What they eat is filled with all the other enzymes, co-enzymes, co-factors and related bioflavinoids that the body needs to function—the true vitamin C complex. When a person eats whole foods with active, fresh nutrients, the body can get along with far less of the essential vitamin than the RDA.

It is also important to remember that the RDA is not intended to be the optimum level of daily intake; it is simply the minimum level on which we can exist (as determined by testing only a few individuals). Unfortunately, the actual RDA varies by bird, species, disease, activity and stress level.

Further, although the number of vitamins has remained constant for years, our knowledge of what we really require in our diets for optimum health has changed. We now call a number of chemicals "conditionally essential." This means that researchers can't discover why we need these chemicals in all situations, but conditionally essential compounds have been shown to treat or cure various maladies.

This means that the list of important nutrients grows longer all the time. Almost all the growth in this knowledge is the result of human research. If we are learning more all the time about the needs of people, how can we even begin to think we know what a bird's needs are? We must shift our thinking away from the stale concept of essential vitamins and minerals in a diet and replace it with the concept that different whole foods supply living nutritional complexes.

We recommend that you fortify your bird's diet with whole-food supplements. These products come from food sources, have no chemical vitamins and are gently processed to retain as many of their nutrients as possible. You can determine whether a product falls into the correct category by looking at the label of the supplement. If it names lots of food products you recognize, it is from whole foods. If most (or even some) of the ingredients sound like a lesson in chemistry, the product is synthetic.

Again, remember that the best way to provide our birds with a multitude of nutrients is to give them juice, fresh foods and variety—not chemical supplements.

JUICING FOR HEALTH

Fruits and vegetables have two components: the fibrous, mostly indigestible component and the juice within the cells of the plant. Only the juice within the cells provides the vitamins, minerals, proteins, fats and carbohydrates we need to thrive. Juicing concentrates these wonderful nutrients into a readily digestible liquid. We recommend that you feed the pulp as well as the juice for added nutrition. Birds usually consume juices readily and in much larger quantities than they would fruits. This makes juicing the best way to provide many of these valuable nutrients.

Because the fibrous component is also important for a healthy digestive tract, continue to feed some whole fruits and vegetables as well. You can also take the pulp from the juicer and feed it to your birds, adding it to other food items mixed into the same bowl.

When juicing oranges, remove the orange part of the peel because it contains indigestible oils. Always use the whitish portion of the peel because it contains a number of extremely valuable bioflavinoids.

Only your imagination limits what you can do with a juicer. If you put nutritious-but-less-tasty products through the juicer, add something tasty like an apple or a pear to improve its appeal to your bird. Feed the juice fresh daily; storage diminishes the nutritional content. If you must store it, pour the remaining juice into an ice tray and freeze it. This gives you a bird-size serving that will defrost quickly.

JUICING RECIPES FOR THE BIRDS—AND YOU, TOO!

Carrot Delight

1 carrot
1/3 of an apple
a few grapes (dark-skinned grapes
   are best)

An Apple a Day

1 apple
1/3 of an orange
1/3 of a banana

Eat Your Broccoli

A few pieces of broccoli
1/2 of an apple
A slice of peeled lemon
1/2 of a pear
A few sprigs of parsley
1/2 of a fresh apricot

Fruit-Juice Mania

1/2 of a ripe banana
1/2 of an orange
Several dark-skinned grapes

The Body Cleanser

1 carrot
1/4 of a cucumber
1/4 of a beet
A sprig of dandelion
A slice of apple
A piece of Shiitake mushroom
   (soaked overnight in a little water;
   don't drain the water when adding
   the mushroom)
A clove of garlic

The Immune Booster

A sprig of dandelion
A sprig of fresh thyme
1/2 of an apple
1/3 of a carrot
1/2 of an orange and white pulp

Liver-Aid Cocktail

1 carrot
1/3 of a beet
2 sprigs of dandelion
2 sprigs of parsley
1/4 of a celery stalk

Breeding and Baby Feeding (Feed to the parents as part of their diet; don't give to baby birds.)

1 carrot
1 kale leaf
1/3 of an apple

The Intestinal Healer

1/2 of an apple
2 tbsps yogurt
1 tsp aloe vera juice
2–3 leaves of spinach
1 tbsp cooked rice (with water added
   in equal portions, left overnight in
   refrigerator before using)
1 tsp apple cider vinegar

VARIATIONS IN GENERAL DIET RECOMMENDATIONS BY TYPE OF BIRD

Different groups of birds need distinct diets. The available foods vary in different parts of the world, and a species will adapt to what it is used to eating. Birds that become successful in an arid habitat such as a dry savanna can flourish and reproduce on the food and water sources found there. As we said earlier in this chapter, little is known about nutritional needs for each species. The suggestions we make here are our best guesses, backed up by our observations and those of other knowledgeable bird owners. We can't begin to cover all the different types of birds and their various nutritional needs, but we have included some of the more common ones, especially birds that often develop health problems as a result of nutritional deficiencies.

CANARIES AND FINCHES

The common species of Canaries and Finches are primarily seed-eaters, and seed should make up about 50 percent of their daily diet. The seed should be a mix of smaller seeds such as rape seed, niger, poppy and millet. Alternatively, many Canaries can learn to eat a formulated (pelleted) diet. You need to be cautious if you try to convert a Canary or a Finch to pellets because it could become sick if it refuses to eat for even a couple days.

Although some aviculturists maintain it is true, there is no justification for believing that these birds remain healthy when fed 90 percent or more seeds. The rest of the diet should consist of fruits and vegetables (25 percent), whole-grain products such as rice (15 percent) and legumes, cooked eggs and yogurt (the final 10 percent).

The rest of the Passerines are a highly diverse group. Some eat seed; others eat nectar, fruit, insects or some of each. Some species of softbills (some Finches and Sparrows, for example) need live animals in their diet such as mealworms and crickets. (If your bird requires this kind of food, we recommend that you breed your own crickets and grow your own mealworms or buy them from commercial sources you can trust for high-quality pet food. Instructions for growing mealworms are included in Appendix C. You can order crickets from retailers with instructions for growing your own.)

Because we cannot cover the best way to feed every species, we recommend that you study several different bird species carefully before acquiring one. Buy one only after you understand the specific diet it needs for optimum health. Find a source for the special food(s) before you buy the bird.

MYNAHS AND TOUCANS

A variety of different birds including Toucans, Toucanettes, Aracaris, Birds of Paradise and Mynahs is susceptible to hemochromatosis (or iron-storage disease), a severe liver condition. It is unclear whether these birds are genetically inclined toward this health problem or whether it is primarily caused by a diet that fails to meet the needs of the species. We do know that we can lessen the incidence of this problem by feeding them correctly. A low-iron diet lowers the incidence of iron-storage disease. Mynahs and Toucans both should be fed a diet consisting mostly of fruits (including papaya, apples, pears and grapes), some vegetables, and a good protein source (animal proteins are optimum). If a formulated diet is fed to the bird, the iron content should be less than 150 parts per million, and it must not make up more than 50 percent of the total diet. Dog and cat foods and monkey chow are often higher in iron than they should be. Never feed these birds dried fruit (including raisins), spinach, monkey chow, certain commercial bird pellets or dry dog or cat food.

Vitamin C increases the absorption of iron, so you should limit citrus fruits in their diets. Raisins and grapes are also high in iron and should be avoided. Never feed these birds organ meat, especially liver; it has a high iron content.

A whole-food source multiple vitamin and mineral supplement can be added to the soft foods daily. Mice or other meat should be added to Toucan diets.

Lories and Lorikeets

Diets for these birds are poorly understood. In their natural habitat, they eat fruits, nectar, pollen, flowers, grass sprouts and possibly some insects. The long-standing recommendations for lories include the basic diet of nectar formula: one teaspoon evaporated milk and one teaspoon honey mixed with one cup of water. It is preferred that you use one of the various commercial Lory nectar diets with the addition of many fruits and some vegetables.

Fresh juices are excellent for these birds. Use a juicer routinely for these nectar-eating birds. Make juices of various combinations of apple, orange, banana, apricot, pear, carrot, kale and broccoli for Lories.

There is a concern about the contents of the various commercial nectar formulas. Some have a high content of simple sugars such as sucrose and dextrose, but wild Lories eat complex sugars, which are certainly better for them. It is common for Lories to have candida infections. This is probably due in part to commercial Lory diets. Other commercial diets seem to be better and have more complex carbohydrate sources and better protein sources. They often have synthetic vitamins added, however, and may contain preservatives as well.

It seems likely that Lories need more fiber in their diet than what is commonly available from commercial nectar. Lories with gastrointestinal disorders (yeast infections, poor digestion, "gram negative" bacterial infections) can be treated successfully by adding a combination of soluble and insoluble fibers to their diets. In addition, Lories that have chronic gastrointestinal disorders usually benefit from a more acidic gut. We recommend Lory nectar diets with psyllium and beneficial yeast, which converts sugars into lactic acid and gently acidifies the gut. Use a "super green food supplement," an antioxidant combination product and a trace mineral supplement as well.

Macaws

Wild Macaws have been observed eating large amounts of high-fat nuts, at least during certain times of the year. For this reason, we encourage people to feed their Macaws more raw nuts than we would recommend for other species. Good nuts to consider include pine nuts, walnuts, almonds and macadamia nuts.

Young Macaws, notably Blue and Gold Macaws, can suffer from hypervitaminosis D_3 (an overdose of vitamin D_3), which can destroy the kidneys and lead to gout. Gout is caused by too much uric acid in the blood. The uric acid crystallizes in the joints of the feet, resulting in swollen, painful feet. Always be careful to avoid feeding your bird too much vitamin D_3.

As with other birds, these birds enjoy fresh vegetables and fruits along with a protein source.

Budgerigars

Too many Budgies (Parakeets) eat a seed-only diet, which they don't do well on. If they are forced to subsist only on seeds, Budgies may suffer from fatty liver disease (hepatic lipidosis), chronic respiratory diseases, renal tumors, gout and obesity. They, more than most birds, need to be convinced to eat a variety of foods.

We recommend that you take a Budgerigar off seeds *gradually* and then begin feeding it a formulated diet instead. (Refer to our ideas about how to wean a seed addict.) Always supplement a formulated diet with fresh foods. We have the most success feeding the "mash" form of the Harrison's certified organic bird diets.

This Budgie enjoys some leftover pizza, but it should also eat fresh, whole food.

Cockatiels

Cockatiels seem to do well on a higher portion of seeds than any other hookbill or parrot-type bird. You should still feed them vegetables and fruits each day, however.

Cockatiels are known for laying eggs repeatedly—even when not breeding—which can endanger their health. Egg formation requires larger amounts of calcium, but keep in mind that Cockatiels are sensitive to high levels of calcium when combined with vitamin D_3. According to *Avian Medicine: Principles and Application* by Ritchie, Harrison and Harrison,

"Adult diets containing over 1 percent calcium, particularly when accompanied by excessive amounts of vitamin D_3 (over 2,000 ICU/kg dry diet) have been found to be excessive in long-term feeding studies." It is best to feed egg-laying hens diets plentiful in calcium-rich foods rather than calcium/vitamin D_3 supplements.

AFRICAN GREY PARROTS

African Grey Parrots seem to crave meats, so we recommend that you feed them a little bit of meat three times a week. African Grey Parrots can suffer the effects of hypocalcemia if they eat a diet containing insufficient calcium. Emphasize the previously mentioned fruits and vegetables that are high in calcium.

AMAZON PARROTS

Amazons seem to be "meat and potato" birds more than other psittacines. They love starches, fats, sugars and salts. Unfortunately, they become obese easily and are always fighting the "battle of the Amazon bulge."

Most Amazons will happily eat table food all the time, rounding out their diet with high-fat nuts and seeds. Owners often are not aware of which foods are nutritious. They may mistakenly think that if they feed their bird spaghetti, pizza, meat, muffins, donuts, crackers and chips, they are feeding their companion a varied diet of fresh table foods. This could not be further from the truth for Amazons or for any bird.

Instead of feeding your bird what it wants, we strongly urge you to feed it the good-quality foods that we have listed.

ECLECTUS PARROTS

Eclectus Parrots seem to need a large amount of fruits and vegetables. We advise against feeding your Eclectus a diet with lots of fats and proteins. They thrive on foods such as carrots and yellow and orange squash.

Many other species also seem to benefit from a diet rich in beta-carotene, which results in a better immune system response to disease. This is yet another reason we recommend feeding fresh foods, "super green foods" and vegetables daily.

EGG-LAYING HENS

Egg production requires a hen to use large amounts of her body's calcium. All female birds that begin laying eggs need increased calcium in their diets, a need best met by adding appropriate foods such as carrots, cabbage, kale, endive, beans, apricots, figs, grapes, almonds, hazelnuts, tofu, eggs and cheese. Their diets should also contain higher fat and protein levels as well.

The Fat Bird

Some bird species have more energy-efficient bodies with lower metabolisms than other birds. These species generally originate in arid habitats where food can be scarce. If fed fat-rich diets or diets that include too much food and too little exercise, these birds can gain excessive weight and compromise their health. Some of the birds in this group include Budgerigars (Parakeets), Galahs (also called Rose-Breasted Cockatoos) and Lovebirds. Budgerigars and Galahs originate on the savannas of Australia. Many Lovebird species originate on the dry grasslands of Africa. These birds must sometimes fly great distances to find food and are often faced with finding food under drought conditions. Low metabolism is a survival technique their bodies have developed to help them use comparatively little food to survive.

Other birds become obese because they willingly adapt to the sedentary lifestyle of most pets. They sit around all day, dipping into a full food bowl without much effort at playing or getting into mischief. Some Amazon Parrots also fit into this category.

Obesity is a major health problem in many pet birds. The only way to help these birds is to feed them diets lower in total calories. They simply must not be allowed to eat as much food as they wish; otherwise, they will stay fat. An obese bird on a diet will probably scream and perhaps will bite you in frustration at not getting all the food it wants. You must weather this storm; eventually, the bird will get used to the limited diet.

Limit nuts, sunflower seeds, safflower seeds and peanuts. Feeding an overweight bird more vegetables and whole-grain products will help, but this technique cannot solve the problem alone.

As with a human on a diet, the rule of thumb is to feed overweight birds good food, just less of it. All the food items we have mentioned are good foods. Remove nothing from the bird's diet unless your avian veterinarian recommends it.

You must reduce the total amount of food you offer. Unfortunately for your bird, this means the food bowl must remain empty much of the day. It does no good for you to lower the fat content of your bird's diet if you let it eat everything else it wants. With free access to full food bowls, your bird will remain overweight. You have to limit the total amount of calories you feed your bird throughout the day.

Birds that fight what we humorously call the "battle of the bulge" should be weighed weekly using a gram scale. Find out from your avian veterinarian roughly how many grams overweight your bird is. You will then know how much weight it should lose. Try to help your bird lose 1 percent of its body weight weekly until it reaches its optimum weight. A bird that is 500 grams overweight should lose between 5 and 10 grams weekly, a safe and manageable goal.

FEEDING YOUR FLOCK: HOME-COOKING RECIPES FOR THE WHOLE FAMILY

It can be difficult to plan and cook recipes strictly for your bird. It is considerably easier to cook dishes for your family that also suit your bird's nutritional needs. The following recipes have not been tested to be nutritionally complete. They are not meant to comprise either your total diet or that of your bird; they are simply meant to help you see how easy it is to create meals that are healthful and delicious for both you and your bird.

Also remember that these recipes can easily spoil if left in your bird's food cup for more than three hours. After feeding, remove the food cups within a couple of hours.

Spaghetti

1 package whole-wheat spaghetti noodles
1 large (19 oz) can of garbanzos, with
    liquid
1 red bell pepper, diced
1 green bell pepper, diced
1 garlic clove, minced
1 cup onion, minced
3/4 cup celery and leaves, chopped
3 cups chopped tomatoes

Olive oil
Water
1 small (6 oz) can of tomato paste
1 bay leaf
1/8 tsp Cayenne pepper
1/2 tsp dried oregano or about
    1/4 tsp fresh, to taste
Parmesan cheese, to taste
Salt, to taste

Drain the garbanzos, reserving the liquid in a large measuring cup. Mash the garbanzos slightly. Mince, cut and chop all fresh vegetables. Add only enough olive oil to a heavy pan to cover the bottom. Heat. Sauté fresh vegetables until they are clear. Add the garbanzos. Add enough water to the garbanzo liquid to make 2 1/2 cups. Add the garbanzos and their liquid to the rest of the ingredients. Simmer for about 2 hours. Serve on spaghetti with Parmesan cheese. Add salt to individual taste after it's served. This recipe freezes well.

Vegetable Lasagna

1 cup zucchini squash, cubed
1 cup yellow summer squash, cubed
1 cup red bell pepper, cubed
1 cup green bell pepper, cubed
2 cups sliced mushrooms
1 cup broccoli, chopped
1 cup carrots, shredded
Olive oil

3 tbsps chopped basil, fresh or dried
2 cups Italian tomatoes, chopped
2 cups tomato sauce
3 cups low-fat cottage cheese
2 cups grated, low-fat mozzarella cheese
1/4 cup Parmesan cheese
1 lb lasagna noodles (if available, use
    whole wheat or vegetable noodles)

Sauté the zucchini, summer squash, bell peppers, mushrooms, broccoli and carrots in only enough olive oil to cover the bottom of a heavy pan. Add basil at the last minute. Stir. Cool.

Mix chopped tomatoes with tomato sauce. Mix cooled, sautéed vegetables with cottage cheese, mozzarella and Parmesan cheeses.

Cook the lasagna noodles according to package instructions. Drain and cool. Add a small amount of olive oil to the water in which you cook the noodles to prevent them from sticking to each other.

Spray the bottom of a rectangular, glass baking pan with a thin layer of olive oil substitute. Pour 1 cup of the tomato mixture onto the bottom of the pan. Alternate layers of sautéed vegetables, tomato mixture and cheese with noodles. The last layer should be vegetables, tomato mixture and cheese.

Cover with foil and bake at 350°F for about 45 minutes or until warm throughout with cheese melted. Let it sit for about 10 minutes before you cut and serve. This dish freezes well.

Tofu Stir-Fry

1 cup brown rice
1 tsp Oriental sesame oil
2 tsps minced fresh ginger or
    1/4 tsp powdered ginger
2 cloves garlic, minced
1/4 cup green onions, sliced thin
1 cup celery, chopped
2 cups carrots, shredded

1 cup snow peas, sliced thin
1 cup green bell pepper, shredded
1 lb firm tofu, cut into small cubes
1 tbsp low-sodium soy sauce
3/4 cup low-sodium chicken broth
2 tsps cornstarch
2 tsps water
1/4 cup pine nuts

Prepare all vegetables and tofu for cooking by slicing, shredding and chopping. Begin cooking brown rice. Heat the oil to a medium temperature in a wok or a large skillet that holds heat evenly. Add the ginger, garlic and onions and cook for about 1 minute. Stir as it cooks.

Add the celery, carrots, snow peas and bell pepper. Stir for about 1 minute. Add the tofu, soy sauce and broth. Cover and simmer for about 2 minutes. Vegetables should remain firm. Remove the mixture to a bowl. Mix the cornstarch with water. Stir well. Add this to the wok or skillet. Stir constantly as the mixture thickens. Add vegetable-tofu mixture to the cornstarch. Mix in the pine nuts. Serve over brown rice. Birds enjoy stir-fried Chinese food over rice. You can get creative in this area.

GRAINS

Grains are a good source of iron, B vitamins, carbohydrates and fiber. They are relatively inexpensive and are versatile. They make a good base for many recipes for any meal, especially breakfast with your bird. Look for barley, bulgar, cornmeal, cracked wheat, hominy grits, kasha, millet, rolled oats, steel cut oats, quinoa (in several colors), Basmati rice, long-grain brown rice, long-grain white rice, wild rice and wheat berries. Cook according to package directions and experiment with the addition of dried or fresh fruit and nuts. Keep in mind that dried fruits often are rich in iron and are unsuitable for Toucans, Toucanettes or Mynahs.

Millet Porridge

1/2 cup shelled millet seed (available at
    health food stores)
1 cup water

1/4 cup dried apricots, finely diced
1/2 tsp lemon zest
1 pinch salt

     Put all ingredients into a small saucepan. Bring to a boil for 1 minute. Cover and simmer for 15 minutes until soft. For a different taste, cook the millet in apple juice and add dried apples or raisins. You can get creative with this breakfast treat.

Brown Rice Cereal

2 cups brown rice
1/4 tsp nutmeg
1/4 tsp allspice
1 quart water
1/2 cup dried figs, dates, raisins,
    peaches or apricots, chopped

1 apple, shredded with skin (remove
    seeds, please)
Pinch of salt

     Add rice, spices and water to a medium saucepan. Bring to a boil. Reduce to low heat and cover the pan. Cook for 40 minutes. Add the dried fruit and cook for 5 more minutes. Remove the mixture from heat and add shredded apple.

     You can be creative with many breakfast cereals, cooking them in juices and adding a variety of fruits and toasted nuts. If time is short in the morning, cook the basic cereal and freeze it for later use. Just before breakfast, warm the cereal in the microwave and add the fresh fruits. For this purpose, you can use cornmeal, Bulgar wheat, rolled oats, wheat berries and couscous.

Uncooked Fruit and Grain Cereal

1/2 cup dried apricots, chopped
1/2 cup cored apple, shredded
1 cup apple juice
2 cups rolled oats
1/4 cup wheat germ or sesame seeds

3/4 cup plain yogurt
1/4 cup honey (for human
    consumption only)
1/4 cup almonds, toasted

Mix the fruit, juice and oats together. Let the mix sit for about 30 minutes. Top with wheat germ or sesame seeds. Serve to your bird with enough yogurt to moisten.

Mix in the rest of the yogurt and the honey to your own taste. You can add almonds or, when in season, you can add fresh blueberries or strawberries.

Carrot-Millet Muffins

3/4 cup rye flour
3/4 cup whole wheat flour
3/4 cup corn meal
2 tsps baking powder
1 tsp baking soda
1/2 tsp salt
1 large egg
1 large egg white

1 cup plain yogurt
1 tbsp brown sugar
1/2 cup dried fruit, chopped (dates,
    apricots, figs, raisins or currents
    work well)
1/4 cup fruit juice
1 1/2 cups carrots, shredded
1/4 cup millet

Coat a muffin pan with nonstick spray or add muffin papers to each cup. Stir together all dry ingredients in a bowl. In another bowl, add the egg, egg white, yogurt and sugar. Mix until blended well. Stir in fruit, fruit juice, carrots and millet. Blend with the dry ingredients.

Add 1/4 cup of the batter to each muffin cup. Bake at 400°F for about 20 minutes. Insert a toothpick into the center of a muffin to test for doneness. The toothpick should come out clean when the muffin is ready.

Muffin recipes lend themselves well to healthful additions that taste good. Experiment with your favorite recipes and ingredients. Jalapeño peppers, for instance, make a tasty addition to cornbread muffins. Your birds will love them, and so will you.

You can improve yeast breads by mixing in sesame seeds, millet, pine nuts, walnuts, almonds and lemon peel. Spice up cornbread stuffing with nasturtium blooms.

Sweet Potato Pancakes

6 slices of sourdough bread, dried
1 3/4 lbs sweet potatoes or yams,
    shredded
2 extra large or jumbo egg whites
4 extra large or jumbo eggs
1 tsp dried chervil

1 tsp cinnamon
1/2 tsp allspice
1 cup nonfat yogurt
4 cups applesauce
1/4 cup blanched, slivered almonds

Reduce bread slices to bread crumbs in a blender or a food processor. Coat the surface of a cookie sheet with nonstick spray. Spread the bread crumbs on the baking sheet and bake for about five minutes at 400°F or until crisp.

Peel and shred the potatoes. In a medium bowl, mix the egg whites, eggs, spices, yogurt, and applesauce. Add the potatoes and almonds. Stir to mix. Add the toasted bread crumbs.

Form into pancake-size circles on the cookie sheet. They must be equally thick from center to edges to ensure that the pancakes will cook evenly. Sprinkle the almonds on top and bake at 400°F for about 45 minutes until crisp on the outside. A toothpick inserted in the center should come out clean when the pancakes are done.

Pizza

1 1/4 tsp active dry yeast
1 cup warm water (105 to 115°F)
1 tsp sugar
1 cup rolled oats (not instant)
1 cup whole-wheat pastry flour
White all-purpose flour
1/2 tsp salt
1/4 cup hulled sunflower seeds or millet
    (optional additions to crust)
3 cups chopped Italian tomatoes
1 tsp fresh basil, chopped (or to taste)

2 cloves garlic, minced
1 tsp fresh oregano
2 cups low-fat mozzarella cheese,
    shredded
1/2 cup Parmesan cheese
1 cup mushrooms, sliced
1 red bell pepper, sliced
1 yellow bell pepper, sliced
1 fresh jalapeño pepper, sliced thinly
    (optional)

Combine the yeast with the warm water and sugar. Set aside for five minutes until bubbles rise and yeast dissolves. Mix dry ingredients together in another bowl. Whirl in a blender until course flour is formed. Mix with the yeast and water. Mix by hand or in a food processor to make stiff dough. If necessary, add white flour to make the dough the right consistency. For texture, add millet or sunflower seeds. Knead the dough for about seven minutes by hand on a floured surface or use a dough mixer until the dough is smooth and elastic.

Coat a bowl with nonstick spray. Place the dough in it. Spray the top of the dough and cover it with a towel. If you live in a dry climate, use a slightly moistened towel. Let the dough rise in a warm place for about 30 minutes.

While the dough rises, mix the chopped tomatoes, basil, garlic and oregano. Let the dough sit. When the dough has doubled in size, punch it down, turn it onto a floured surface and knead it again for about 5 to 10 minutes. Form it into a round or rectangular shape, depending on the pan you use. (A cookie sheet will work as well as a pizza pan.) Stretch it until the pizza dough is about the same thickness from edge to edge. Let it rise for about 10 minutes, covered in a warm place.

Cover the surface of the dough with the tomato sauce. Next add the cheese and toppings. Get creative with toppings. Almost any vegetable is good on pizza. If you want, you also can add crab for a bit of a different taste. Avoid cured meat such as pepperoni, ham and salami. These are unhealthy for you and your bird. Bake at 450°F for about 20 minutes in a preheated oven. If you are in a hurry, use prepared refrigerated or frozen dough.

Beans and Rice

1 1/2 cups white or brown rice	1 yellow onion, chopped
Olive oil	3 garlic cloves, minced
6 stalks of celery, chopped	2 cups black beans, cooked
1 red bell pepper, chopped (save tops and seeds for your birds)	2 cups red beans
	1 cup tomatoes, chopped
1 green bell pepper, chopped (save tops and seeds for your birds)	3 cups low-sodium vegetable stock
	Chili pepper to taste
1 jalapeño pepper, finely chopped	

Begin cooking the rice. Brown rice takes about 40 minutes to an hour to cook. White rice cooks in about 20 minutes. In a large skillet, heat about 1 tablespoon of oil and sauté the celery, peppers, onion and garlic until soft. Add the beans, tomatoes and vegetable stock. Simmer for about 40 minutes. You also can add shredded or sliced carrots, mushrooms and cilantro to this dish. Serve over rice. If you want, you can garnish with plain yogurt.

LEGUMES AND BEANS

Beans and legumes are excellent sources of protein, vitamins and minerals. Birds eat cooked beans readily. The following is a brief listing of beans you can find at your grocery or health-food store. Many of these beans and legumes are sold dried. They can be rehydrated for cooking using two methods.

The first method requires the least amount of time. Place the beans in a large pan and cover them with about 2 inches of water. Bring this to a boil. Cook for about two minutes. Turn off the heat. Cover the pot with a lid. Let the beans sit for an hour. Cook according to package directions.

The longer method may reduce intestinal gas and is just as easy if you plan. Cover the beans with 2 inches of water and let them stand overnight (or about eight hours). Cook according to package directions.

- Black beans (also called black turtle beans) have magnesium and protein.
- Garbanzo beans (also called chickpeas) are rich in protein.
- Lentils are high in protein and folacin, a B vitamin.
- Pigeon peas are a good source of protein.
- Pink beans contain complex carbohydrates, folacin and magnesium.
- Pinto beans are high in protein, magnesium and iron.
- Red kidney beans are a good protein source.
- Split peas (green and yellow) are also rich in protein.
- White kidney beans are a good source of protein and iron.

THE ENERGETICS OF FOODS

The Chinese have known for centuries that different foods have different *energetics* in the body, properties that have little to do with the vitamin and mineral content of these foods recognized by conventional Western medicine. Foods can be warming, cooling, heating, bitter or salty. Different foods enter different channels and organs in the body. Knowing which foods act in what ways will help you predict what effects these different foods may have on the body. This section provides some ideas about some common foods and their energetics.

Walnut: *Walnuts are considered to be a Kidney Yang tonic. This means they will be warming and drying to the body. They also tend to support kidney functions, especially those related to the adrenal gland, as well as strength and recovery from long-term illnesses. Walnuts often work best for birds that have chronic diseases, that have wasting conditions such as tuberculosis or that are underweight. Walnuts boost Yang excessively in younger birds, who often already have Yang excess. They add excessive weight as well. Give them to younger birds in small quantities.*

Dandelion: *Dandelion is excellent for birds. It is a Yin tonic and a diuretic. It cleans the system. Find dandelions growing in a field or in your yard that you know have never been sprayed with herbicides. A leaf can be added to any of the preceding recipes. The root can be boiled and the tea* *poured over soft foods. Use no more than a dropper of the tea for each medium to large bird, less for a small bird.*

Egg yolk: *Egg yolks harmonize and moisten the body. They concentrate in the liver and the skin more than anywhere else. They are excellent for birds with active liver disease. This is due in part to the quality of the proteins egg yolks contain, which are healing to the liver. They also are a good blood tonic.*

Milk: *Milk has a downward movement to its actions and produces a lot of fluid and mucous. It is a good tonic for the stomach, but it can often produce excess mucous in the intestinal tract, making it a less desirable food for many birds.*

Sweet potato: *Sweet potato concentrates its actions in the intestines, kidneys and spleen. It is healing to the membranes of the intestines. It is sweet, so it promotes digestion. It also strengthens the kidneys and the lungs. It promotes Yin, so it is anti-inflammatory in nature. This explains why it is good for chronic diarrhea and intestinal inflammation.*

ORGANIC GARDENING

If you have time, you can garden organically for yourself and your bird. If you don't have time, you can buy organic foods at your grocery store. If you decide to try a garden, you can start small and then expand if you enjoy the experience.

Many experienced gardeners who use organic methods refer to their gardens as being self-sufficient. Once a garden of this type has been established, a natural balance occurs that keeps pests under control and plants flourishing—all with no spraying schedules, no worries about the dangers of chemical pesticides and fertilizers, and with larger yields. Initially, you'll have to devote some thought and work to your organic garden, but it pays off in a reduced workload as time goes on. The "Resources" appendix lists some books about organic gardening, or you can consult your local book store.

7

RECOGNIZING AND CATEGORIZING ILLNESS OR INJURY

It is important for bird owners to learn what their bird looks like when it is healthy. This is why we stress the importance of an examination by a holistic avian veterinarian as soon as possible after you buy your bird, preferably on the way home from the pet store or breeder. During this first exam, the veterinarian can talk about signs that indicate the bird's health. Regular well-bird visits to the avian veterinarian are also valuable so the owner can build a base of knowledge and so the veterinarian can become familiar with the bird.

SIGNS OF ILLNESS

We've already covered the early warning signs of problems. Now we'll cover physical signs that may indicate that an illness has developed. If you see these signs, immediate veterinary care is needed. It cannot be emphasized enough that when a bird looks sick it is very ill and may have been sick for a prolonged period. Birds wish to hide their illnesses, and their makeup is such that they suffer from an illness for prolonged periods. Remember that each bird is a unique individual; it won't show the same signs as another bird with the same illness. Some of the sickest birds may show only one or two of these symptoms. Don't be fooled into thinking that things must not be so bad because only one or two symptoms are present.

Sick birds tend to slouch much of the time. They may hunker over with both feet on the perch, and their wings might hang down a little. Early in the disease, when the bird has some strength, it might perch on one foot all the time, trying to rest and conserve energy. Later, it may feel too weak to tuck one leg up and will have both feet on the perch, even when sleeping. The head often is held low down between the shoulders, usually a bit forward. The bird might wish to sleep all the time, taking several naps each day.

The hallmark symptom of a sick bird is a fluffed, huddled appearance, although this is not always seen, especially with the largest birds. A sick bird has trouble maintaining a normal body temperature, so it holds its feathers out to retain as much heat as possible. The fluffed-up appearance may be more prominent along its backbone. After all, when we feel sick, don't we often feel coldest along the back? Caretakers who do not understand what a fluffed-up bird looks like often think their bird has grown larger or heavier.

The bird's droppings might undergo serious, consistent changes. There may be excessive urine or urates in them, or there may be diarrhea. There might be a yellow or yellow-green color change to the urine. Droppings might develop a foul odor. Droppings with seeds or other food in them are an indication that food is passing through the intestinal system undigested. This is a serious sign of illness, as is seeing blood in the droppings.

In addition to the quality and character of the droppings, be aware of the normal number of droppings your bird produces on a daily basis. Although this will vary from bird to bird, your companion should remain relatively consistent. If the number of droppings increases or decreases significantly, there is often a problem.

Breathing may become labored. The bird might start bobbing its tail with each breath. Worse yet, the bird might be open-mouth breathing, fluffed and sleepy. Any sign of breathing difficulties is always of great concern.

The sickest birds often are those that huddle on the floor while they sleep, those that close their eyes all the time, or those that are very weak, can't fly well and even have trouble climbing from perch to perch. Those that keep their heads hanging all the time are critically ill.

All bird owners need to own a gram scale suitable for weighing their birds. When there is more than a 5 to 10 percent weight loss, your bird is sick.

Vomiting is always of great concern in a bird. Birds almost never vomit unless they are very sick. Unfortunately for many caretakers, it can be hard to recognize when they are vomiting. A bird will not projectile vomit; rather, it regurgitates the contents of its crop into its mouth and then shake its head back and forth to remove the food from its mouth. A vomiting bird often looks like it has something pasted to the sides of its head. Its feathers will seem streaked back, or perhaps there will be a little crusty appearance to the feathers on the sides of its head.

There is a difference between vomiting and behavioral regurgitation. Birds will regurgitate for their babies or a mate. If they have a close, loving relationship with you, they may start regurgitation for you. When birds vomit due to illness, they will do it at any time. When they are regurgitating behaviorally, they only do it when they are excited, when they are with you or perhaps when looking into a mirror. (They are regurgitating for their "friend" in the mirror.)

Under the tail around the vent, the feathers might become pasted with feces and urates. This is especially common in weak birds that are sitting on the cage floor and that have kidney disease or diarrhea. Any bird you think might be sick should be turned over to check for this problem. If present, in addition to taking the bird to the doctor, you will have to clean off the vent. Otherwise, your bird may not be able to defecate due to the obstruction the pasted stools cause.

Birds that should have powder down, including African Grey Parrots, Cockatoos and Cockatiels, can lose that powdery feel and look to their feathers. If a Cockatoo or African Grey has lost its ability to produce powder down feathers, its beak will look shiny, and the feathers will tend to look a little greasy. Complete loss of all the powder down is always a serious problem. A milder decrease in the amount may indicate illness as well.

Some birds may exhibit discharges from the eyes, nose or mouth. Learn how to look into your bird's mouth to know what is normal and what is abnormal. Your companion might allow you to open its mouth, or you may need to look when it yawns. Many birds will yawn when you gently rub their ears.

Signs of Serious Illness

- Sleeping all the time
- Fluffed, squinty-eyed, huddled birds
- Seeds and other food items in droppings
- Increases or decreases in the number of droppings produced daily
- Blood in the droppings
- Feces or urates pasted to or around the vent
- Yellow-colored urine and urates
- Loss of powder down
- Tail bobbing, squeaky- or stuffy-sounding breathing, open-mouth breathing or labored breathing
- Marked weight loss
- Egg bound but unable to pass the egg
- Discharge from the eyes, nose or mouth; crusted shut eyes, red eyes or swollen eyelids
- Vomiting
- Any bird that seems disoriented, acts drunk, can't climb around in the cage or huddles on the floor

EMOTIONAL STRESS

A stressed bird will reflect its anxiety in both subtle and overt ways. It may cower in a corner of its cage, or it may strike at anyone who comes near. It may engage in self-destructive behavior such as pulling or shredding its feathers. Even worse, if left untreated or corrected, self-destructive behavior can lead to physical disease.

An emotionally stressed bird will act out in ways that are difficult to ignore. It may scream or bounce up and down endlessly. A normally calm, affectionate bird may suddenly bite unexpectedly or strike and bang its beak on whoever comes near. It might even begin to bite viciously. Your job is to find out why and fix the problem.

Body language is a good indicator of avian stress. A bird with a fanned tail and upraised wings might be in a defensive/aggressive posture. Remember, however, that your bird could simply be playing with you; it's important to know how to read your bird.

Some birds reflect a change of mood in their eyes. Many birds "pin" their eyes when they get excited. The African Grey is a prime example of this behavior—the size of its pupils changes rapidly. When this happens, you need to be on the alert because the bird is frightened, angry or excited. The bird understands the situation from its point of view and is communicating the idea to you. You must then find out what the bird wants you to know. An Amazon Parrot also uses its eyes to indicate its emotional state. When its eyes are light in color and the pupil is dilated, an attack or bite may be imminent.

Many parrots, including African Greys, will "pin" their eyes when they are excited, angry or frightened. This means that the pupils will change sizes rapidly.

Early Physical Signs of Stress

- Feathers that have become frayed or dull, that have changed color or that look unkempt
- Excessive or prolonged molting
- Eyes that have developed redness, that have swollen lids or that look squinty or almond shaped
- The *Shen*, or life force, ceasing to shine brightly through the eyes
- Lessened play behavior
- Sleeping more during the day
- A fluffed appearance, perhaps with a ridge of fluffed-out feathers running up the back
- Plugged nostrils, wheezy breathing or food or feathers sticking to nostrils
- Sneezing or yawning all the time
- Loss of feathers anywhere on the body (a bird should never molt in such as way as to develop bald areas; if the loss of feathers is around the head, it could be sinusitis)
- Changes in water consumption, increase or decrease in appetite
- A consistent change in the look of the droppings that can't be explained by the food recently eaten by the bird
- Smelly and/or watery droppings

Body language is always a good indicator of a bird's emotional state. Many large birds move their head and neck slowly like a snake and hold their wings away from their body as they fan their tail to make themselves look larger than they are.

Because smaller birds are more fearful and are less likely to attack, they may fly about their cage or aviary, bashing themselves against anything in their path.

Emotional stress can easily lead to physical disease. We know that to be true for ourselves. Doesn't it often seem like you become ill when you can least afford to? This often occurs when you have been working overtime developing your new pet project, when your children are having problems at school, when your parents become ill or perhaps when you move into a new home. These are some emotional stresses that can lead to disease for us.

Your bird is no different. If you used to work only part time but have taken a full-time job, your bird will become emotionally stressed. If you bring a new pet into the home, there will be less time for your bird. If you develop a new relationship with someone, the bird will feel neglected; they know you are diverting some of your love and time from them.

Look at the section about proper care for your bird. If any of these needs change (perhaps you have changed the location of the cage in the house), your bird will be emotionally stressed. Emotional stress will lead to behavioral changes. If you act early to correct the stress, your bird won't become physically sick down the road.

A Look at Signs of Emotional Stress

- Feather grooming patterns change.
- Feathers become broken, frayed or fuzzy looking.
- Feathers get plucked out.
- Bald areas develop where there used to be feathers.
- When grooming, the bird looks rushed, irritated, angry or overly aggressive in its grooming patterns.
- Playing lessens or destructive behavior increases ("acting out").
- Your bird starts biting you.
- The bird wants to stay isolated, refuses to come out of the cage or hangs on the side of the cage.
- The bird becomes less vocal or, even more commonly, begins to scream much of the time.

One of the first signs of emotional stress might be a bird that starts to preen its feathers abnormally. Normal preening is a calm, systematic grooming of the feathers. Grooming should make you feel calm when watching your bird do it. Each bird uses a pattern as it moves all over its body.

Birds that are stressed emotionally might develop a frantic, forceful or overly aggressive pattern of preening. When watching them preen, you might start feeling a little edgy yourself. This is because over-preeners are nervous, angry or irritated, and they demonstrate this as they groom. They may keep going back to the same location rather than evenly preening all over. The feathers may become frayed, bent, distorted or discolored from their constant over-preening at the same location.

Look at your bird's interaction with you. Is it normal? Does the bird want the same amount of playtime with you, petting from you and generally the same interaction with you as in the past? Perhaps your bird has become a bit of a recluse, wanting to stay in its cage more frequently. You might see your companion wanting to sit on your shoulder all the time rather than actively playing with you. Maybe you are even getting a few bites when you ask your bird to do things it would usually do. Think of yourself: Don't you tend to get grumpy when overly stressed? Don't you often want to hide out and just be by yourself when your emotions are out of control, when you are frightened or when something is crushing you down or frustrating all the time? When a bird is emotionally stressed, with keen observation, you can see the same behaviors we exhibit ourselves when life has dealt us the emotional "bad hand."

Pay attention to vocalization—a bird that is suddenly less vocal usually has at least some mental stress developing. Even more commonly, emotionally stressed birds start to scream much more frequently. They are frustrated and yet have no outlet to relieve their frustration.

SUBTLE SIGNS OF STRESS

Feathers often reflect stress. In addition to shredded feathers, bald spots are common in stressed birds that preen nervously. The growth of feathers in a stressed bird is often quite different from that of a normal bird.

Stress marks or stress bars can form in a feather as it grows. These marks look like bars of a color different from the rest of the feather, or they may be "lines" made up of spaces. These marks can develop because of nutritional deficiencies as well as from emotional stress. Feather bronzing, a condition in which the normal color is replaced by a dull brown or gray, is another indication that your bird is stressed. If your bird has abnormal feathers, begin to look at the whole situation in which it lives—from diet to exercise and other factors in its environment. You have created the stressful environment, and you must change it.

Other subtle signs include a bird that plays less than usual or that sits listlessly during times when it should be active. Activity level will be unique to your particular bird, and you must know what's normal for your bird. A Lovebird that sits still may be stressed; an Eclectus that sits quietly may be acting normally. No one can know better than you what is normal for your bird. Sleeping more than usual and at abnormal times is another stress indicator. Most birds wake in the morning and remain active until an afternoon nap. After the nap, they remain busy until bedtime and often relax during the evening. Again, the exact pattern is unique to each bird.

A bird that hangs forlornly on the side of its cage is unhappy. Other signs of unhappiness in a bird include constantly climbing in circles around the cage, halfheartedly flapping of its wings as if looking for a place to fly, and trying to find a way out of its cage. If your bird has begun to behave in these ways, it's time to evaluate its overall health and happiness.

Another sign of a stressed bird is the "dancing" bird. People often think it cute when their bird dances back and forth on its perch. In actuality, the dancing is a perverted activity exhibited by a bird desperate to get away from where it is, to go do something else or to find a secure place.

Each bird is an individual, and you need to know what's normal for it before determining if there's a problem. (Eclectus Parrots)

8

TREATMENTS

How does disease arise? Some people remain healthy although they are exposed to potentially harmful bacteria, fungi, viruses and toxins each day, while others seem chronically ill. The truth is that we don't know why humans, birds or other animals become sick. When we look for the causes of illnesses, however, we must include emotions as a major factor.

How many times, when we become sick, are we being adversely affected by some event in our lives? Our child is getting in trouble, the boss at work is unhappy with our performance, our income is suddenly not covering all our expenses, or the in-laws are arriving for an extended visit. These are just a few examples of common problems we might have to deal with in our lives. When we suffer the emotional upheaval these types of problems can cause, our bodies are susceptible to physical illness. We always seem to get sick when we can least afford it because that is when we are most stressed.

THE BACH FLOWER REMEDIES

Dr. Edward Bach recognized the need to improve the emotions as one of several ways to treat disease. He started his research in the 1900s, investigating how flowers might affect emotions. He knew that the sight and smell of certain flowers produced various emotional shifts in humans. Eventually, he learned how to isolate the flower's essence, which then can be used for therapeutic purposes.

He categorized thirty-eight flowers by their ability to alter the emotions of his patients. Flower essences are intended to work only the mental and emotional aspects of the patient. There are flower essences for fear, anger, transition, anxiety, depression, insecurity, stress and many other emotions. Several different flower essences often are combined in the same bottle to deal with multiple emotional symptoms. A flower essence formula is usually used with other therapies.

English flower essences, modeled after the thirty-eight flowers of Dr. Edward Bach, are remarkably effective for various emotional problems. A more common name for them is the Bach Flowers. We know that this is a trade name and that several companies produce essences in the traditional way that can be called Bach Flowers. We will use the name Bach Flowers here in honor of Dr. Bach.

Some animal behaviorists believe that animals do not have emotions. Anyone who has lived with and studied birds knows that birds do have feelings. It can be difficult to determine the emotions that negatively affect a bird, however. We recommend that you closely observe your bird's behaviors and ask yourself what negative emotions are adversely influencing your bird. (Please note that Bach Flowers are to assist in healing your birds. They should not replace conventional therapies that your bird might need.)

RANGE AND LIMITATIONS OF BACH FLOWERS

To use Bach Flowers effectively, it is important to understand what they can and cannot do. They can alter negative or pathological emotions with remarkable effectiveness, but normal emotions and behaviors are not affected. Let's look at Cockatoo behavior, for example. Cockatoos want and need constant attention. Observing Cockatoos in the wild, we see that they will congregate in the same tree. All members of the flock usually perch on the same branch, shoulder to shoulder, all preening each other. They expect this close attention from their caretakers as well.

Many problems Cockatoos suffer in the home environment directly relate to the fact that, as wonderful bird behaviorist Chris Davis said, Cockatoos would love to be skin grafted to your chest. Bach flowers will help calm a Cockatoo when you are not around, but they will never alter the basic need it has for constant attention.

Bach Flowers take time to become effective. They are gentle, effective healers, but they cannot overpower or sedate your bird. They take time to alter the bird's negative emotions. Don't give up if you haven't seen any changes in a few days. It often takes a month or more to see improvement, so persistence in giving the remedies is important.

Use the information later in this chapter to match Bach Flowers to your bird's emotional state. Then select the combination of flowers you believe best fits your bird's needs. Make sure you give the flowers consistently several times daily. It takes time for the Bach Flowers to work, so wait at least two weeks to assess the effect of the flowers you selected.

If there is any improvement, continue the therapy. If you see no improvement in a few weeks, reassess your bird and select a different Bach Flower or combinations of Bach Flowers.

HOW TO DILUTE FLOWER ESSENCES

Bach Flowers come in small vials and are preserved in alcohol. This is the tincture, or full-strength, remedy. Because Bach Flowers work on the energetic level of the body, the strength or quantity of the flower essences does not matter. Swallowing one diluted drop is roughly the same as drinking the entire bottle. Because of the alcohol content, you should never dose birds directly from the tincture; always dilute it first.

Dilute each essence by putting four drops of the tincture into a 1-ounce bottle of spring water. Rescue Remedy is used at double the dose of the other flowers—eight drops into an ounce of spring water. Do not use alcohol as a preservative if you are going to use it with your birds. Remember that the mixture of water and tincture can become contaminated with bacteria. You must keep it refrigerated and avoid touching the tip of the dropper to the bird's mouth, skin or beak or to your own fingers.

Using the Diluted Essence

Place the essence directly in the bird's mouth with an eyedropper that can be washed. Avoid using the dropper that stays in the bottle because the Bach Flower formula could become spoiled with bacteria. Find a spare dropper that can be cleaned between uses. You can add the essence to the bird's water bowl or rub the essence on the bird's beak or feet. You can also spray the bird with a bottle of spring water containing the flower essences. Keep in mind that the skin will absorb the remedies, but the feathers will block the body's assimilation. You must get some of the spray on the bird's feet or face.

Although quantity does not matter, how often you dose your bird does. For long-standing problems, if the problem is not acute and you have time to correct the problem, dose your bird two to three times daily. During acute times of stress or when problems are severe, give your bird the flowers every hour or even every few minutes in the most extreme cases.

ADDING MORE THAN ONE BACH FLOWER TO THE SAME BOTTLE

Emotions are always complex, and it is common to want to combine the effects of several Bach Flowers into one therapy. By reading the rest of this section, you can develop combinations of flowers for every condition.

Most practitioners of Bach Flower therapy believe you can combine up to six or seven flowers into the same bottle but no more. The one exception to this is Rescue Remedy, which has five flowers but counts for only one flower if you decide to add it to you patient's regimen. A careful assessment of your bird usually produces a clear picture of its emotional needs, allowing you to use fewer flower essences at the same time. The fewer you use, the more focused the effect, so you should strive to develop treatment strategies with three to five flowers.

Always work on the most important problem first. Other problems may surface when the first one disappears. Treating with Bach Flowers is often like peeling the layers of an onion. You remove one negative emotion only to reveal a deeper problem, which you then must treat.

RESCUE REMEDY

A particularly effective combination, Rescue Remedy is worthy of separate mention. It contains Star of Bethlehem, Rock Rose, Impatiens, Cherry Plum and Clematis flowers. This formula is beneficial for birds that are stressed, birds that are suddenly scared for any reason or birds that are taken to any new surrounding.

GROUPING FLOWERS

When you try to determine which Bach Flowers or combination of flowers you should use, first study the different flowers and what they treat. Understanding the grouping of different flowers helps tremendously in deciding which flowers to consider. This is why the thirty-eight Bach Flowers are not usually listed alphabetically. Instead, they are commonly listed under categories or headings that indicate the problem they can be used to alleviate. To help you find the flower you are looking for, however, we will start out with an alphabetical listing that shows the category under which each flower falls.

1.	Agrimony	Overly sensitive to influences and ideas
2.	Aspen	Fear
3.	Beech	Overly concerned for the welfare of others
4.	Centaury	Overly sensitive to influences and ideas
5.	Cerato	Uncertainty
6.	Cherry Plum	Fear
7.	Chestnut Bud	Insufficient interest in present circumstances
8.	Chicory	Overly concerned for the welfare of others
9.	Clematis	Insufficient interest in present circumstances
10.	Crab Apple	Despondency or despair
11.	Elm	Despondency or despair
12.	Gentian	Despondency or Despair
13.	Gorse	Uncertainty
14.	Heather	Loneliness
15.	Holly	Overly sensitive to influences and ideas
16.	Honeysuckle	Insufficient interest in present circumstances

17.	Hornbeam	Uncertainty
18.	Impatiens	Loneliness
19.	Larch	Despondency or despair
20.	Mimulus	Fear
21.	Mustard	Insufficient interest in present circumstances
22.	Oak	Despondency or despair
23.	Olive	Insufficient interest in present circumstances
24.	Pine	Despondency or despair
25.	Red Chestnut	Fear
26.	Rock Rose	Fear
27.	Rock Water	Overly concerned for the welfare of others
28.	Scleranthus	Uncertainty
29.	Star of Bethlehem	Despondency or despair
30.	Sweet Chestnut	Despondency or despair
31.	Vervain	Overly concerned for the welfare of others
32.	Vine	Overly concerned for the welfare of others
33.	Walnut	Overly sensitive to influences and ideas
34.	Water Violet	Loneliness
35.	White Chestnut	Insufficient interest in present circumstances
36.	Wild Oat	Uncertainty
37.	Wild Rose	Insufficient interest in present circumstances
38.	Willow	Despondency or despair

FOR FEARFUL BIRDS

Aspen

Aspen, *Populus tremula,* is for birds that are fearful. These birds see unknown threats around every corner. They jump and startle easily. Their fears are often unconscious; the bird often does not know why it is afraid. Aspen is for vague fears of foreboding and apprehension that cannot be clearly defined; Mimulus is for general fears due to known conditions. Because we often don't know whether the bird's fears are of unknown things or known things, we recommend that you use Aspen and Mimulus together whenever there is fear.

You can use Aspen for:

- Fearful birds that jump and startle easily

- Birds that carry excessive anxiety that something bad will happen

- Feather pluckers for which fear of the unknown is a problem

- Cockatiels and other birds with "night fright" attacks, in which they wake up in the middle of the night and fling themselves wildly around in the cage, often injuring themselves

- Cockatoos and African Grey Parrots that are highly suspicious by nature

Cherry Plum

Cherry Plum, *Prunus cerasifera*, is for openness, composure and a willingness to accept our path in life. Birds that might benefit from Cherry Plum feel that all of life is threatening them and that disaster is around every corner. This emotional state is exhibited mostly as being completely out of control. In its worst manifestation, the bird might react to this fear by attacking others "before they attack me."

Birds that are constantly attacked by other birds or routinely threatened by dogs or cats often develop this negative outlook. Others that are placed in front of a window—being trapped inside a cage where they can't escape from the threats they perceive outside—may need Cherry Plum.

You can use Cherry Plum for:

- Birds that have fear, especially fear of losing control

- Birds that lose control or suddenly become vicious, attacking with little provocation

- Self mutilators and any bird that bites, chews or scratches itself—especially when seeing something it fears or dislikes yet feels it can do nothing about

- Self-mutilating birds; birds that bite and chew themselves

Cherry Plum is used to treat fearfulness and proactive aggression.

- Birds that need to remain in control when strangers are around or when they are placed in unknown environments; birds that are boarded while the owner is away

- Birds that become frantic when traveling in the car or to the veterinarian

- Growling African Grey Parrots and screaming Cockatoos that are reacting to strangers

- Boarding Birds

Mimulus

Mimulus, *Mimulus guttatus*, is for confidence and courage and to drive out fear. It is often said that Mimulus is for known fears, or tangible fears, while the Bach Flower Aspen is for unknown fears. We often use Aspen and Mimulus together when fear is present because it can be hard to determine whether a bird is suffering from known or unknown fears.

Consider using Mimulus for:

- Birds that are fearful of strangers, new toys, new cages, new drapes or furnishings in their room

- Treatment of long-term fears and long-standing phobias

- Birds that are being picked on by mates or by other birds in the house

- Timid, reserved and shy birds

Red Chestnut

Red Chestnut, *Aesculus carnea*, is for birds that worry about others to the point of failing to worry about themselves. They have great concerns for others but fail to see to themselves. They often fear the worst for those they worry about.

Consider the use of Red Chestnut for:

- Birds that are anxious about their owners being gone, hanging on the sides of the cage all the time (Note: Many birds with this behavior actually need other remedies because this behavior can arise from different emotions.)

- Birds that only pluck when their caretakers are away, especially when they are away longer than the bird expects

- Baby birds that are removed from their parents (Rescue Remedy is another option in this situation)

Rock Rose

Rock Rose, *Helianthemum nummularium*, is for courage and strength, especially during stressful times and times of crisis. Those that need Rock Rose believe they are in danger both mentally and physically. Rock Rose is the remedy you should reach for during emergencies. Rock Rose is for panic and anxiety that rapidly turns into terror.

Rock Rose is one of the remedies in Rescue Remedy. It can also be combined with one or two other flowers depending on the situation. Rock Rose can be combined with Clematis, for example, when a crisis has led to a near coma state. Rock Rose can also be combined with homeopathics such as Arnica and Aconite depending on the case.

Rock Rose can be used for the type of chronic fears we see in birds that are always being bullied by another bird or person in the house. This leads to adrenal gland exhaustion, which can create immune deficiencies.

Although Rock Rose is a classic remedy for acute problems, it can also be used in some chronic conditions. Rock Rose helps with addictive behaviors that have developed due to long-standing fears. It also is for the bird that feels as if it is out of control of its life.

Use Rock Rose for:

- Terror, cage-fright episodes, attack by cats and so on

- Panic that has set in for any reason

- Birds that have developed "cagosis" due to fear and terror

- Some types of feather-grooming disorders that have developed from terror, fear or panic

- Help in strengthening will and developing the courage to meet the day's problems head on; for a bird abused by its mate

- Birds being constantly picked on or beaten up (physically but also mentally)

- Birds for which fear develops into Yang deficiency and adrenal gland stress

- Known terrifying events such as fireworks celebrations

FOR BIRDS THAT SUFFER UNCERTAINTY

Cerato

Cerato, *Ceratostigma willmottiana*, helps a bird accept its judgments as valid. On a more spiritual level, Cerato relates to an understanding and acceptance of one's higher self and calling. Those needing Cerato often ask others for advice all the time, never trusting their own intuition. This leads to a lack of attention to life.

Although it can be difficult to determine which birds need Cerato, we might think of using it for:

- Birds that lack adequate attention spans or are mentally flighty

- Birds that don't learn things easily because of inattention to life's lessons

- Birds that imitate others instead of forming their own behaviors and ideas

- Birds that fail to wean on time

- Birds that don't trust people or other birds because they fail to rely on their own judgments about who is caring and who is untrustworthy

To Improve Confidence

Gentian

Gentian, *Gentiana amarella*, is for despondency and discouragement. It helps restore confidence after long-term setbacks with a known cause, as opposed to Mustard, which is used when the cause is not identifiable. On a more spiritual level, Gentian is related to faith in the world and in one's own place in it.

We might use Gentian for:

- Birds that have a chronic disease, such as allergies or gout, especially during times of flair-ups when the disease worsens

- Any setback

- Birds that do not have enough confidence and faith in themselves and their ability to perform their tasks; breeding birds that don't successfully hatch and rear their young

- Recovery from depression caused by known circumstances

Gorse

Gorse, *Ulex europaeus*, is for hopelessness and despair. It helps when a bird has given up on life or has lost any faith that its lot could improve.

Gorse might be used for:

- Chronically ill birds that seem to have lost the will to fight on

- Feather pluckers that seem depressed or unhappy

- Birds battling illnesses from which they might not recover (such as cancer)

- Birds that have anemia due to chronic disorders, to rally their bodies so they have hope of becoming healed again

- Birds that need a positive outlook on life, to place a "ray of sunshine" into their lives

Hornbeam

Hornbeam, *Carpinus betulus*, is one of the remedies for birds that suffer uncertainty. More specifically, it provides the mental and physical strength to complete tasks that seem too difficult. It is used to provide inner strength and vitality; we often use it to counter exhaustion.

Hornbeam is less commonly used in companion animals than in people because it is for mental exhaustion, a state more difficult to determine in a bird.

It might be used for:

- Birds that have had a prolonged illness, to strengthen the exhausted mind more than the body

- Birds that have led a boring life for years, caged all the time and with few toys

- Show and performing birds, to counter the emotional drain they may experience

Scleranthus

Scleranthus, *Scleranthus annuus*, produces balance, equanimity and composure. It is for those who vacillate from moment to moment or day to day about the mental, physical or emotional aspects of their lives. Birds with rapid mood swings might benefit from Scleranthus. It is beneficial during moments of chaos when the world is shifting around us rapidly. Scleranthus can bring calm and reason to an uncertain time. It helps bring forth decisions when they are needed. Birds that need Scleranthus are often quiet and reserved. They hold their indecisiveness within.

As with many Bach Flowers, determining the emotional events that lead to unhealthful actions can be difficult, but we might use Scleranthus for:

- Physical problems such as following seizures

- Equilibrium problems (Note: Bach Flowers are available to assist in healing your birds, not to replace conventional therapies they might need. Most birds that have balance problems are severely ill and need immediate veterinary medical attention.)

- A bird that has flown into a window

- Birds that seem to have rapid mood swings, happy one moment and then unhappy the next; offer it only when there is no cause for the mood changes

- A bird that needs to focus on the task at hand

- Balance, the Yin and Yang of life (physical, emotional or mental)

- Balance of a bird's hormonal swings

- Feather pluckers that pick during breeding times

- One-sided problems: only one foot has a rash, weakness on one side and so on

- Birds that need help learning to fly, especially rehabilitated baby birds that seem clumsy; birds that fall off swings and ropes all the time

Wild Oat

Wild Oat, *Bromus ramosus*, relates to purpose, goals and achievement. In the negative state, the individual bird that benefits from Wild Oat—although intelligent, reasonably ambitious and gifted—will lack purpose. The individual has only a vague understanding of what he or she should be doing.

Birds that suffer uncertainty in their life might benefit from Wild Oat. Breeding birds, if offered several nest boxes, will move from one to the other and never decide which one to select. Many birds in a home or aviary situation have no definable tasks and find nothing to occupy their day. This lack of purposefulness may eventually lead to behavioral problems.

Wild Oat can be used for birds that:

- Have some feather-grooming problems, especially overpreening birds, when they seem to drift through life without a focus to their daily activities

- Cannot decide which nest box to select, which mate to select, what toys to play with and so on

- Are trained to perform, to help them focus on their tasks

- Need help to focus on the task at hand

- Are breeding

- Are bored, to help them focus on life

FOR INSUFFICIENT INTEREST IN PRESENT CIRCUMSTANCES

Chestnut Bud

Chestnut Bud, *Aesculus hippocastanum,* is for birds that do not seem to learn the lessons of daily life. They develop a lot of regret because they always repeat errors. There is great stress in their lives.

You can use Chestnut Bud:

- To improve mental activity and the ability to learn lessons

- To improve training

- To break bad habits

- To help birds that have trouble acclimating to a new home

- To help wild-caught birds that fail to adapt to an aviary or a home situation

Clematis

Clematis, *Clematis vitalba,* is for birds that live in a world of their own, not caring about others. They are reserved, withdrawn and uncommunicative with others. They are often sleepy and may even have chronic illnesses. This is due to a lack of caring and effort at the physical, spiritual and emotional aspects of life.

We might use Clematis for:

- Chronically ill birds, to strengthen them and help lead them toward healing

- Baby birds that need added vitality and strength, especially those that are runts or are weak due to any cause

- Help in awakening birds from anesthesia more rapidly and bringing birds back from a comatose state

- Slow-developing baby birds, to stimulate growth

- A bird that needs to focus on the tasks at hand, especially during training

- Birds that seem to sleep too much

- A bird that needs to develop a more lively interest in life and those around it; Budgies and other birds that have become addicted to mirrors or toys

- A bird that needs to become well-grounded and emotionally stable

Honeysuckle

Honeysuckle, *Lonicera caprifolium*, is for birds having trouble letting go of the past. They often live with great regret and sorrow over what life was but is no more. As a result, they are no longer happy with their lives. Honeysuckle is used for wistful regret but not actual guilt for wrongful past actions. (This state is seen in Pine.)

Birds that might need Honeysuckle include:

- Those that have lost a loved one—not for the sorrow and loneliness but for the regret—to replenish mental and physical strength

- Birds that have lost their mates and will not accept new ones

- Birds that need the best remedy for homesickness

- Birds sold into new homes; birds that are homesick

- Birds that are left at a veterinary hospital and long to go home

Mustard

Mustard, *Sinapis arvensis*, is used to bring back cheerfulness and a positive outlook on life. It can remove depression and melancholy. Those needing mustard suffer from a detachment from life with resulting depression; the cause of the depression is often not known. Mustard is in the insufficient-interest-in-life category. We tend to use Mustard for depression combined with a desire to isolate oneself from the surrounding world.

Mustard can be used:

- By spraying mist in a room to remove depression when a traumatic event has occurred (such as a bird dying)

- For birds that seem to like to be alone all the time, especially older, cranky birds

- When seasonal breeding behaviors are exhibited as irritability and a desire to be alone

Olive

Olive, *Olea europoea*, brings peace and calmness after a difficult time. It restores balance and improves the spirit. Olive is often needed most when our birds have reached the end of their mental and spiritual endurance, when exhaustion has brought them to the point of collapse. Olive improves the will to live in sick birds.

We might use Olive for:

- Exhaustion from a severe ordeal, such as when a bird has been trapped (behind the refrigerator, for example) and physically traumatized

- A bird that fractured its leg and remained alone until you came home at the end of the day to find it huddled on the cage floor

- Birds with chronic skin problems, allergies or autoimmune skin diseases, to give them strength to carry on

- A wild bird that has been caged in an attempt to rescue it, but the bird continues to thrash around

- A bird that needs focus to continue a difficult task, to add reserve strength when exhausted

- Any bird fighting a severe illness, to give it the will to live

White Chestnut

White Chestnut, *Aesculus hippocastanum*, produces tranquillity and peace of mind. In the negative state, we see those needing White Chestnut as being unable to relax because the mind is racing away, unable to make decisions. Thoughts just keep circling around with no letting up or resolution. This mental turmoil is often brought about by events in our day that come back to bother us later, never allowing us peace of mind.

This mental turmoil is hard to determine in birds, but we might use White Chestnut for:

- Birds that seem normal sometimes but are nervous and unsettled at other times

- Birds that have trouble going to sleep at night

Wild Rose

Wild Rose, *Rosa canina*, is for birds that are unhappy because they don't care about life anymore. This is usually caused by constant frustration; they do not think they can change their lot in life. They lose interest in the present, but more than that, they lose interest in trying to change the present.

Many birds can benefit from Wild Rose. Birds are essentially wild animals that have been brought into confinement. Many are left in cages too long throughout the day. They are not given any tasks to perform, and they have no ability to improve their lot in life. Eventually, they will lose interest in trying to change their life and will mope around listlessly. This lack of interest and hope can lead to behavioral problems or physical health problems. With no interest in life, the will to live often leaves, and chronic illness may set in.

Consider using Wild Rose:

- For birds that live in close confinement and are unable to achieve their goals, leading from frustration to apathy

- For chronically ill birds to build up their desire to live

- To help a bird be more content with a home, cage or aviary situation when they really would rather be outside in the wild

- To help a bird remain reasonably happy when forced into a situation it does not like:

    When a bird is placed in a cage with another bird it does not like

    When a bird lives with a caretaker who must be gone from the home for twelve hours a day or more

    If a bird must live around young children that may annoy it

FOR BIRDS THAT SUFFER FROM LONELINESS

Impatiens

Impatiens, *Impatiens glandulifera*, is for loneliness. This loneliness arises from a bird's desire to work by itself because it wants to get things done right away. The bird is unable to work with others because they do not move as fast as desired.

Impatiens is also for mental nervousness and all types of physical nerve conditions, such as the following:

- To provide serenity and patience when things are not going the bird's way

- For nerve disorders with the following signs of impairment: headaches, leg paralysis in Budgerigars (along with other therapies), nervous twitches, foot stomping, or "cageosis" behaviors

- For any type of pain

- For nervous birds, when the nervous state is brought on by a desire to get things going and to complete the task ahead

- For male Cockatoos in breeding season

Heather

Heather, *Calluna vulgaris*, is for loneliness. Birds that need Heather think only of themselves to the point of using others to solve their problems. They need to be the center of attention all the time. They have a strong dislike of being alone. A strong characteristic of the negative Heather state is that the bird lives off of the energies of others, sapping its strength in the end.

This can be hard to determine in birds because they are naturally flocking animals and thus do not wish to be alone. In other words, it is a normal and healthy emotion for them to want to be with others. The matter of degree, however, determines whether the behavior is pathological or normal.

Some of the conditions we would consider using Heather for include:

- Birds that pluck feathers only when they are alone

- Birds that must be the center of attention, always needing to jump into the middle of everything to gain attention

- Birds that play tricks on you or that destroy things just to get your attention

- Birds that have already exhibited the negative state of Heather (give it to them whenever their caretaker is gone or they are boarded)

- Birds that bite you when your attention is elsewhere (although this can be normal behavior for many birds)

- In mated pairs, when one of the pair always asks for the preening, constantly demanding attention and feeding by a mate

Water Violet

Water Violet, *Hottonia palustris*, is for loneliness. Animals that benefit from Water Violet want to be alone when sick and when healthy. They tend to be self-reliant and independent, perhaps overly so. They are confident and competent. In the negative state, they have no humility and instead would rather be alone; they tend to be haughty.

Their confidence and individuality can make them feel alone and unattached to those around them. Others see this air of confidence and may tend to burden them with demands and tasks. Their air of confidence is mistaken for being aloof and having disdain for others. Over time, this may make them rigid and more withdrawn.

Water Violet can be used for:

- Birds that like to be left alone when sick

- Birds that are unafraid in a cage and are not necessarily aggressive nor submissive, but when paired with a mate, they sit away from the other bird, refusing to even consider a relationship

- Birds stricken by grief (this is one of the best remedies for grief) following the death of a mate or the loss of their human companion (or even just separation from either)

- Birds exhibiting signs of loneliness and isolation

FOR BIRDS OVERLY SENSITIVE TO INFLUENCES AND IDEAS

Agrimony

Agrimony, *Agrimonia eupatoria*, is one of the better flowers for birds. It is common for pet birds to live in an alien environment that is less desirable than they would choose. Birds that benefit from Agrimony try to ignore the negatives in their life and suppress these feelings. They always exhibit a positive outlook to their caretakers and the world in general.

This suppression, in its early stages, leads to restlessness and a search for peace. Later, it may lead birds to behave in ways that are extremely detrimental toward themselves. Caretakers often say that their bird is always happy, and they don't understand why the bird has become a feather picker or self-mutilator. Birds that need Agrimony rarely bite their caretakers; they prefer to agree to whatever others ask of them. Many chronically ill birds develop this state because of the stress they place on themselves by suppressing their basic needs.

As you can see, suppression with a cheerful exterior can lead to significant mental, emotional or physical illness. These are the hallmarks of birds that can benefit from Agrimony.

Agrimony might be of benefit for:

- Feather pluckers, especially self-mutilators

- Allergic conditions and nonspecific dermatitis with secondary self-trauma

- "Cageosis," when a bird can't find a comfortable place and climbs around in the cage, bobbing its head up and down; birds that "dance" all the time

- A bird's inability to adjust to captivity and a caged life

Two homeopathic remedies that immediately come to mind for this type of bird are *nux vomica* and *tuberculinum avium*. These remedies are for the pathology exhibited in the patient which often arises from suppression of emotion.

Centaury

Centaury, *Centaurium erythraea*, is another useful flower for birds. Centaury is for birds that don't stand up for themselves. These birds let themselves be pushed around, always consenting to what their owners or other birds want rather than determining what they want. Individuality is sacrificed to the needs or desires of those around the bird. Centaury adds a little "backbone" and strength of character.

In some ways, Centaury is the most important flower for strengthening the soul or spiritual aspect of life. Centaury strengthens us so we can more easily reach out for life's goals. Many people are taught bird-training methods that are really domination techniques. People are often told by behaviorists that they must be dominant and that the bird should never "get its way." For further discussion of this issue, see Chapter 3, "The Emotional Bird." Centaury will help correct the damage caused by this ill-conceived training technique.

We might consider using Centaury for:

- A bird with no will to live

- Birds that seem to try to please their owners at all costs

- Birds that "step up" even when they are doing something they like (and are being asked to do something else by a person they don't like)

- Birds that are always chased away from the feeding bowl by other birds

- Any bird kept in a cage all the time that rarely gets out to enjoy playtime

- Budgies addicted to their image in a mirror or to a specific toy (to help them gain the strength to venture out of their cage)

One homeopathic remedy that has many of the characteristics of Centaury is Silicea.

Holly

Holly, *Ilex aquifolium*, is one of the most important flowers; it will be of value to all of us at some time in our lives. Its positive aspect is that of love, nurturing and caring for and about others. Birds that fail to receive the love they give can become angry. They feel abandoned, separated and forsaken. There is a lot of jealousy in the negative Holly state.

Birds that might benefit from Holly include:

- Any bird that displays jealousy

- Birds that show fits of anger including biting their caretaker and attacking strangers who come into the house

- Birds that need to feel more love, nurturing and protection from the harsh world around them (such as birds in quarantine, birds in pet stores that do not promote a protective environment, and birds whose caretakers are away on trips)

Walnut

Walnut, *Juglans regia,* is one of the more useful flowers; it eases birds through transitions. It is commonly needed but usually only for brief periods of time when our lives are changing and events around us put us in turmoil. Birds that need Walnut are often overly sensitive to the outside world and are easily influenced by others. Walnut helps individuals adjust to new surroundings. It protects us from the negative influences from the world around us. Individuals that need Walnut often are tied to the past because they are hypersensitive to new things and are unstable during times of change.

We might use Walnut for:

- Birds that need to adjust to a new home, cage or cage mate
- A bird that has lost its mate or human caretaker (to help settle the bird in its new life)
- A bird with a fear of loud noises, children, dogs or thunderstorms
- A bird that needs stability during changing times
- Birds with chemical sensitivities

FOR DESPONDENCY OR DESPAIR

Elm

Elm, *Ulnus procera,* is for individuals overwhelmed by responsibility. It helps restore a sense of balance and calmness to those who are usually stable and well-adjusted but become unbalanced due to the pressing concerns of life. It can help restore serenity after unusually difficult circumstances. Elm is usually used only briefly because the negative state is not prolonged. Use Elm for birds that are overwhelmed by responsibilities or that have temporary self-doubt and exhaustion, real or imagined.

Elm might be used in the following situations:

- For birds that are flying or traveling
- For birds in a new home or aviary

- To restore a bird's emotional balance after it has been temporarily overwhelmed
- For birds that have just had their first clutch hatch or pip
- For birds entered in a bird show
- Following beak and nail trims or exams at the veterinarian
- During holidays, when strangers "invade" the bird's home

Crab Apple

Crab Apple, *Malus pumil,* is used as a cleansing remedy—physically, emotionally and spiritually. Crab Apple is for acceptance of oneself and those around us. Crab Apple helps treat despondency and despair, especially when these emotions arise from a negative opinion of ourselves. There is an unclean feeling of mind or body, a poor self-image. Crab Apple can be used as a cleanser, internal or external.

We might use Crab Apple for:

- Birds that are suffering from poisonings such as heavy metal poisonings or pesticides
- Feather-grooming abnormalities in which self-mutilation has caused secondary bacterial or fungal skin and follicle infections
- Birds that have been attacked by a cat (also consider Rescue Remedy)
- Draining infections anywhere
- Part of a detoxification plan, either routinely or for sick birds
- Birds that have been rescued from the wild, especially when there are feather lice present, chronic infections or bumblefoot
- Any bird that seems to mope around in the cage, overpreen and not play with toys

Larch

Larch, *Larix decidua,* is used to build confidence and remove despair. It is for those who feel inferior. People should take Larch before any test or stressful event in which they have to stand on their own and perform. For yourself, Larch may be a great remedy to take before attempting anything you see as a challenge such as a test or perhaps an interview.

In cases needing Larch, there often is a lack of self-confidence. The bird won't even try and is sure of failure.

For birds, consider using Larch for:

- A Cockatoo that cowers in its cage

- A bird that tries to climb on top of its owner's head when faced with strange people or events

- Abused birds, to regain self confidence

- Despair, when repeated traumatic incidents have sapped all strength

Oak

Oak, *Quercus robur*, is used to add strength; it enables one to fight on. Oak, being in the despondency and despair group, is intended to bring about our potential for strength and endurance.

Those who need Oak always seem to struggle with life. Oak aids birds that try to get well from chronic illness. Oak also is good for parent birds that give too much of themselves as they raise one clutch after another. Oak is most appropriate when the spirit is good but the task is difficult.

We might use Oak for:

- Birds that have been physically abused for some time, to build strength

- Young birds that are stunted in size and birds that have not been fed well

- Baby birds that have been improperly hand-fed and weaned

- Birds that have been chronically ill and are now in the recovery stage

- A bird that has lost its mate while feeding babies, to give strength and almost superhuman endurance

Pine

Pine, *Pinus sylvestris*, is for regret and forgiveness. Those who can benefit from Pine often are ruled by guilt. Pine is for those who lack an appreciation of life because of guilty feelings that can lead to a feeling of rejection and to blaming oneself for all the problems in life.

The emotions of birds can be hard to read. It is difficult to tell when a bird feels guilty, blames itself for everything and is never content with its efforts. Think about using Pine when a bird seems depressed and its mood worsens when its caretaker is in an unhappy mood. The bird may think it is the cause of the problem.

Guilt depletes energy, as does self-reproach, a feeling of unworthiness. Those that benefit from Pine always blame themselves.

In the despondency and despair group, we might use Pine for:

- A bird that reacts with guilt whenever its caretaker is upset, even though the bird has nothing to do with the problem

- A bird that has trouble developing a relationship with a mate, and you suspect the problem is due to feelings of inferiority

- Abused birds that feel they caused the abuse and that they deserved the abuse because they are not worthy

- Abandoned birds

- Birds that are unfortunately relegated to back rooms because their owners believe that they are too messy or noisy

Star of Bethlehem

Star of Bethlehem, *Ornithogalum umbellatum*, is perhaps the most beneficial of all the Bach Flowers. It is used to repair all untoward effects of trauma: mental, physical and emotional. Trauma can produce adverse consequences for years after an incident. Star of Bethlehem is indicated for all the effects of trauma—not only those apparent immediately after the trauma, but effects that can appear years after the inciting incident as well.

Star of Bethlehem is perhaps the most important component of the five-flower Rescue Remedy, and it is used most often as part of this combination. Traumatic episodes often lead to despondency and despair, and Star of Bethlehem is effective for these negative emotions. It brings comfort for the worst cases of unhappiness and sorrow, even when those affected do not want consolation.

There are many instances in which a bird could benefit from this flower. For the most severe and clear-cut situations, you can give Star of Bethlehem alone. Usually, however, you will use it as a part of the five-flower Rescue Remedy. Other effective combinations include: Star of Bethlehem, Clematis and Crab Apple following anesthesia and surgery when there is a slow recovery; Star of Bethlehem, Holly, Crab Apple and Wild Oat for birds that have experienced some deep-seated emotional shock and have continued to have physical or emotional problems; Star of Bethlehem and Walnut for newborn chicks, especially those with assisted hatches; and Star of Bethlehem and Pine for abused birds that have been rescued from the abusive situation.

Birds that might benefit from Star of Bethlehem include:

- Those that have suffered from cat attacks, fireworks, car accidents and other traumatic incidents

- Birds grieving after the death of a mate

- Parent birds that have had their clutch removed for hand feeding

- Birds that have been separated from their life-long human caretaker when sold into a new home (or any other similar event)

- Birds that need to be returned to a calm state after an angry outburst by their caretaker, especially if the birds have been struck or physically abused in other ways

- Birds suffering from any type of trauma

- Birds needing comfort and solace

Sweet Chestnut

Sweet Chestnut, *Castanea sativa*, is for the worst feelings of despair. It is used when we are in a hopeless, self-destructive mood, when we have reached our limit and there is nothing else to do.

Birds that might benefit from Sweet Chestnut include:

- Those that have been in a crate flying to a new home (feeling like they are completely trapped and will never get out again)

- Any bird that lives with an abusive bird and cannot get to the food and water

- Birds that live in front of a window, watching a falcon fly overhead or cars that flash reflected sunlight into their eyes (feeling at their wits' end, unable to do anything to improve their lot in life)

Willow

Willow, *Salix vitellina*, is for resentments. Those that need Willow want to blame everyone but themselves for their problems. This leads to despondency and despair.

Willow is for those who suffer adversity and repeated frustrations but cannot understand why it is happening to them. They are unable to accept these setbacks; instead, they complain and blame others. The problems they encounter may be real or imagined; the key is that the individual becomes resentful and unhappy. The individual may end up acting out this resentment in destructive ways.

Because resentment leads to despondency, Willow might be a good remedy for a depressed bird, even though you may not know whether resentment is the cause of the depression.

Remember, when a bird's resentment is justified because you have been ignoring it, the best thing to do is give it some of your time.

We might consider using Willow for a bird that:

- Is acting out in resentment when it screams, tears up its cage, escapes from its cage and destroys the house

- Ignores you after you have been gone all day

- Approaches you later and gives you a little bite to let you know it is unhappy

- Only starts to pluck feathers when you come home

FOR THOSE OVERLY CONCERNED FOR THE WELFARE OF OTHERS

Beech

Beech, *Fagus sylvatica*, might be effective for a bird that shows a lack of tolerance. This lack of tolerance, although usually emotional, can also be a lack of patience for physical things such as allergies, temperatures and other changes to its physical environment. Beech enables us to be more open minded and to look at the world around us in a positive way.

We might recommend Beech for:

- A bird that doesn't want to change its diet to one that is more well-rounded (seed addicts and picky eaters)

- An African Grey Parrot that plucks feathers when the furniture is moved

- A bird that won't accept a new toy out of fear

- A bird that is intolerant to heat and cold or that has allergies to ingested or inhaled substances

- The bird that refuses to accept a new mate

- An Amazon Parrot that attacks a new roommate, child or spouse

- Birds that hold themselves rigid on the perch, unyielding to the emotions that should sway them

Chicory

The negative state of Chicory, *Cichorium intybus*, relates to overcaring that often leads to overbearing, domineering attitudes. These birds are strong willed and demand that the other members of the household behave in the way they wish them to behave.

We might use Chicory for:

- Birds that overpreen or pluck the feathers of other birds

- Birds that control the behavior of their mates

- Domineering birds

- Birds that demand attention all the time

- Birds that are overly possessive of their owners, driving away all others

- Birds that are unable to be away from their human companion

- Birds that have chronic sinus infections with stuffy breathing and congestion

- Birds that need help letting go of a lost person or other bird

Vervain

Vervain, *Verbena officinalis*, is about self-discipline and restraint. Animals that need Vervain are not directed toward their own goals as much as they need to be; instead, they are too concerned about the needs of others. Vervain is in the overcaring for others group and is used to stabilize an individual, to bring calm and peace and to root the individual into the present tasks at hand. Birds that need Vervain are often high-strung. They are nervous because they have firm ideas about how things should be and are unable to make the world bend to their "superior knowledge." They want everyone to convert to their views.

We might use Vervain for:

- Birds that are unable to focus on the present, that keep pacing around, bobbing up and down, even when their caretaker is with them

- A mated pair in which one bird always dominates the other one, telling it what to do and where to go

- Birds that won't stop vocalizing, even when their caretaker is present and giving them attention

- Birds that try to dominate all residents of a home, chasing people around, making the dog leave the room and keeping other birds off play toys

Vine

Vine, *Vitis vinifera*, is often used for strong-willed individuals that carry power and authority. Those that need Vine often are too domineering and tend to boss others around. They are self-assured and dictate to others due to a sense of purpose. Those that need Vine want to dominate the home and have a purpose in what they do to achieve their goals.

Both Vervain and Vine are in the overly concerned for the welfare of others group. Vervain is for a domineering, high-strung bird; Vine is for a domineering bird that is not particularly high-strung. Those that need Vine are deliberate in their domination; those that need Vervain are overly enthusiastic about trying to achieve their goals. Vine types calmly go about getting what they think is needed. A personality that needs Vervain is flighty, edgy and bossy.

Birds that might benefit from Vine include:

- Any bird that wants to own the house

- The bird in the aviary that bosses all others around

- Birds that need purpose and resolve (such as before competitive events or to focus new parents on the task of raising their chicks)

Rock Water

Rock Water, *Aqua petra*, is the only remedy that is not a plant. It comes from natural springs in pristine areas and is known for its power to heal the sick. Those that need Rock Water are too rigid in their lives and are unwilling to accept change; they are stubborn and unyielding. They are creatures of habit and determination. They often forsake the joys of life, opting instead to work. They often are the "nose to the grindstone" type that needs to do things themselves.

These individuals often want to force changes in the world around them to meet their idea of what is best for the "common good." Rock Water personalities always know what is right for everyone else and don't hesitate to tell everyone. The key to Rock Water is that the individual has a compulsive need to perform tasks and does not deviate from what is "right" in a humorless pursuit of what they perceive is the greater good.

We might use Rock Water for:

- Birds that seem stubborn and unwilling to open themselves to new behaviors

- Birds with behavioral problems such as screaming, plucking or circling in the cage when their human companion is not present (thinking they must be with their person to manage things and keep everything in order)

- Stiff, arthritic birds

- Older birds that have become too rigid in the goings on of life

- Birds that refuse to modify their eating habits, that eat only certain food items and refuse anything to which they are not accustomed

- Birds that reject any new toys in the cage; even more so, birds that do not like changes in the home, fearing for their owners

- Birds that dominate their mates, demanding that they do what is "right" all the time

HOMEOPATHY

WHAT IS HOMEOPATHY?

According to the World Health Organization, homeopathy is the second most popular form of health medicine in the world today, surpassing traditional Western medicine. In France, 32 percent of family physicians prescribe homeopathic medicines. In England, 42 percent of medical doctors refer clients to homeopathic physicians.

Homeopathy is popular because it is free of side effects and is remarkably powerful. It is not a synonym for holistic medicine; rather, it is its own brand of health care. It is a form of medicine far different from Western medicine. It is based on the principle that "like cures like," an idea that has been recognized for centuries. Patients are treated with medicines that, when given in large doses, create the same symptom pattern as the disease being treated. Homeopathy can be defined as a system of medicine in which diseases are treated by drugs capable of producing, in healthy people, symptoms like those of the disease being treated, although the drug is administered in minute doses. In contrast, Western medicine practices allopathic treatment, in which symptoms are treated by drugs that produce different symptoms than those being treated. To prevent adverse side effects, homeopathic remedies are highly diluted. To enhance the remedy, they are "succussed," or shaken, during the dilution process.

To practice homeopathy at its highest level, we need to understand the principles of how it works, how to select remedies, what potencies of remedies to use and how frequently to use them. This is beyond the scope of this book. We will, however, cover a few remedies that can be used in emergency situations and for certain other common problems.

How to Dose and Select Remedies

Always select low-potency remedies such as 6X, 12X, 6C or at most 30C. Many health-conscious stores carry these remedies. We believe that, for most situations, it is best to use single-remedy products. This is called "classic homeopathy." Remedies are supplied as single potencies and with one remedy to a bottle. A less common and less effective method of homeopathy is to use multiple remedies and multiple potencies in the same product. You can tell when a homeopathic product has multiple remedies by looking at the label. It will list several different remedies, often with different potencies. The problem with giving multiple remedies at the same time is that the body is given mixed signals about how to go about healing itself. The end result is, at best, only a superficial level of healing. Single remedies, when correctly selected, give the body a clear and strong signal for how to heal itself.

Remedies often come as pills, which are hard to give a bird. You can place several pills in your bird's drinking water, enabling the bird to receive its dose when drinking. (You must never place anything else in the same water.) Alternatively, you can place several pills in a glass dropper bottle filled with spring water and give your bird drops in its mouth from the dropper. Giving your bird drops of the homeopathic remedy is the best method, but it can't be used with birds that are too wild.

You might dose your bird once or twice daily or, if it has severe problems, several times daily. With higher potencies, it is common to give only one dose daily or perhaps even one dose each week. With emergencies, we often give the remedy several times daily, perhaps at hourly intervals until the bird is better or we have gotten the bird to the veterinarian.

There are hundreds of remedies, any one of which might be the best one for your bird. The problem with homeopathy is that ten different birds, each having what appears to be the same disease, might be treated with ten different remedies. This is due to the subtle differences in the pattern of signs with each sick bird. The psychological and emotional picture that makes up your bird is just as important as the physical signs of illness. Thus, you will find that we commonly mention mental and emotional signs when we talk about the remedies.

It takes years of study to accurately prescribe remedies. For any significant problem, it is always best to consult a veterinarian trained in homeopathy. The list provided covers only a few remedies and provides a very general idea of when to use them.

How Soon Should the Remedy Work?

Western allopathic drugs immediately make a change in the body by lowering the fever, relieving pain, stopping the diarrhea and so on. They enter the body and immediately change the way it is functioning. Although this form of medicine might offer immediate relief of symptoms, there often is no healing going on. The symptoms often return when the medication wears off (such as blood pressure medicine you take three times daily, every day).

Homeopathic remedies don't work that way. Unlike allopathic drugs, homeopathic remedies don't alter the way the body is functioning. They enter the body and support the way it is trying to heal itself. They don't make the body do anything different. They gently guide the body to effectively heal itself. This takes time, so homeopathic remedies usually don't work immediately. They often work over the course of days, weeks or even months. The speed with which they work is entirely related to the time the body needs to heal itself. We wouldn't expect a fractured bone to heal in less than six months, would we? As the body heals itself, symptoms may become worse for a while. After all, the body's symptoms are often occurring because that is how healing takes place. When a remedy is given, the patient often becomes a little sicker. This is called a homeopathic aggravation. In other words, it is good to see this result as long as the overall appearance of the bird is a little better.

A HOMEOPATHIC *MATERIA MEDICA* OF COMMONLY USED AND EMERGENCY REMEDIES

A *Materia Medica* lists the remedies and how they work. A complete discussion of any one of the following remedies would take several pages; anyone wishing greater depth of information should consult a complete *Materia Medica*. This list will highlight some of the emergency uses for the remedies listed.

Aconitum Napellus

Aconitum is often used in cases of great fear, shock and mental collapse. Although it is very good for these conditions, it is equally effective for deep phobic conditions. You can use it for birds that have night frights all the time, those that have a great fear of thunder, and those that thrash around in their cage uncontrollably when frightened.

Arnica

Arnica is perhaps the most commonly used remedy. It is wonderful for trauma of all kinds. When we see bruising, we think of Arnica, but it is just as good right after a sprain or fracture. If your bird flies into a window, think of Arnica. If it gets a leg caught in its cage, use Arnica. It is also a good selection right after any other type of injury. What is less known is that Arnica is just as good a remedy immediately following any type of mental or emotional trauma. Give Arnica for two to three days after any traumatic episode. We usually recommend a 30C potency two or three times daily. Perhaps a 6C or 12X potency could be used hourly, if necessary.

Homeopathy for Feather Grooming Disorders

Feather grooming disorders are common in companion birds, primarily psittacines. You will find information on the treatment of feather grooming disorders in several sections of this book, including here as well as in the Traditional Chinese Medicine and Nutraceutical Therapies sections.

Abnormal feather grooming includes plucking feathers, over preening or chewing feathers, excessive scratching and rubbing of feathers, and self induced dermal lesions such as feather folliculitis and dermal abrasions. Most grooming disorders are speculated to be due primarily to behavioral causes such as sexual frustration, fears and boredom. Secondary pathological changes to the dermis and adnexa worsen the grooming disorders. These include traumatically induced feather folliculitis, bacterial folliculitis, bacterial dermatitis and pruritus.

Homeopathic remedies have proven helpful in controlling and treating feather grooming disorders. The most successful, however, is usually a combination of homeopathy, nutrition, nutraceutical and Traditional Chinese Medicine for these cases.

Feather grooming disorders are among the most difficult problems in birds to treat. This is due primarily to the lack of "work" the typical bird has in a domestic situation. In the wild, a bird's day is filled with tasks to perform from sunrise to sunset. In a home or aviary almost all of the natural tasks necessary in the wild are gone. This leaves our birds with little to do throughout the day. Some adapt to this better than others.

The ones that do not adapt as well often are those that develop chronic illnesses, "cageosis" behaviors (for example, birds that incessantly bob up and down on the perch, what owners often call "dancing"), and feather grooming disorders.

A smaller percentage of the birds will have internal diseases, which predisposes them to develop abnormal feather grooming. These include allergies, infections, and degenerative organ diseases such as hepatic lipidosis. Every bird that has feather grooming disorders should have a complete exam and diagnostic panel from an avian veterinarian.

Remember, many of the skin changes or skin diseases the avian veterinarian diagnoses are actually secondary to the "psychological" aspect, although they often need to be treated as well. This means that if any bird digs at its feathers excessively, secondary skin infections and feather follicle infections will occur. It common terms this called the "itch, scratch, itch" cycle where the more we scratch, the more we itch. This is due to the inflammation caused to the skin and feather follicle by the over preening and plucking, which leads to more abnormal grooming behaviors.

Other western diagnoses, such as the commonly diagnosed "giardia," only rarely if ever cause feather grooming disorders. As we have mentioned in the paradigm section of this book, some western diagnoses are really only a categorization of symptoms, and do not get to the root cause of the problem. This is not to negate the positive effects seen from western pharmaceuticals, and we are not necessarily recommending against their use. But, if the bird continues to pluck, a holistic minded veterinarian needs to be consulted.

Some birds pluck as part of a perverted reproductive drive. It is our belief that they are particularly good parents (or perhaps just compulsive parents!), and have a strong drive to find a mate, nest build and rear young. These birds pluck mostly during their breeding season. This type of plucking is harder to treat using homeopathy in our experience. Herbal medicine and especially acupuncture for these cases can be used. Our only goal with these birds is to moderate their behavior, because the basic reproductive drive they are displaying is not psychologically abnormal.

Western medicine may treat these seasonal pluckers with hormonal therapies and tranquilizers. Some hormonal therapies are relatively safe, like chorionic gonadotropin (HCG), while others are very dangerous, and the progesterone, testosterone, and estrogen therapies fall in this category. Drugging a bird for an essentially normal behavior somewhat troublesome. Only rarely the use of what we call psychoactive drugs (such as Prozac) are used for the same reason. Other therapies employed include a variety of tranquilizers, which have proven ineffective in my experience.

Collars may be indicated with some birds, especially those that are causing extensive damage to their skin from chewing. In rare cases they are used with birds that are early in their plucking and chewing behaviors. Collars do nothing to improve the underlying condition. However, they can protect the feathers and skin while holistic therapies are instituted.

In combination with homeopathy, we often use Bach flower therapy. Look in the section covering the Bach flowers, which we call English Flower Essences in this book.

The following is a system that can be used to treat "psychological" feather grooming disorders using homeopathy.

Good Remedies in General

Examples of commonly used homeopathic remedies for feather grooming disorders:

- aconitum napellus
- apis mellifica
- arnica montana
- arsenica album
- belladonna
- ignatia
- natrum muriaticum
- nux vomica
- pulsatilla pratensis
- psorinum
- sepia
- staphysagria
- stramonium
- tuberculinum avium
- veratrum album

There are well more than 600 remedies to choose from and any one of them might be the right remedy in the individual case. This list is intended to get you started looking for the right remedy. We often find success with remedies not in this list. Although you might find the correct remedy form this list, perhaps what probably will be more helpful would be to use these remedies to guide you in the study of homeopathic therapy for mental problems. By studying natrum muriaticum, for example, you will be led to other remedies that have somewhat similar effects. This will give you more ideas on which remedy to consider with each case.

Remedies By Groups of Psittacine

Certain birds are the most common to present with feather plucking disorders. There may be a group of more commonly indicated remedies within each group of birds, due to commonality of personalities within groups of birds. There are significant differences from bird to bird, and any bird could easily not fit into the generalizations below. The patients own signs and symptoms is always needed to determine the best remedy.

Cockatoos: Cockatoos are very social birds. In the wild, they are often seen congregated together in one tree, and with several birds side by side on the same perch. They need close contact, and it has been said that they would love nothing more than to be "skin grafted to their caretakers chest." A lot of their problems are due to the lack of the intimate social contact and social and sexual interactions between themselves and other cockatoos.

Remedies that are more indicated in cockatoos include:

- chamomilla
- ignatia
- natrum muriaticum
- nux vomica
- pulsatilla pratensis

Amazons: Amazons are often sick from systemic diseases, and the plucking is only a part of the problem, so a complete work-up is always in order (as with all birds). They seem to have a lot of hormonal problems as well. If the problem becomes only "psychological", consider:

- nux vomica
- sepia
- sulphur
- veratrum album

If their problem is more seasonal and hormonal, consider:

In female Amazons:

- aconitum napellus
- apis mellifica
- calcaria carbonica
- chamomilla
- lycopodium clavatum
- pulsatilla pratensis
- silicea
- sulphur

In male Amazons:

- apis mellifica
- camphora officinarum
- cantharis
- conium maculatum
- nux vomica
- staphysagria
- tuberculinum avium

African Grey Parrots: African Grey Parrots are usually plucking from emotional or mental reasons. They are highly emotional and very intelligent animals and need caring and knowledgeable care-takers to provide for their needs. Their need for remedies is extremely broad as they can have most of the same problems that people experience! We still have only marginal success with African Grey pluckers, due to the depth and variability of their emotional and mental disease. Their owners should probably be treated at the same time as the bird, if we are to have great success with them (something we, of course, can not do!). Some remedies to try might include:

- nux vomica
- pulsatilla pratensis
- ignatia
- arsenicum album
- stramonium
- natrum muriaticum
- phosphorus

Eclectus Parrots: Eclectus parrots seem to chew out of boredom and from sexual frustration, thus remedies for abnormal sex drive and sexual frustration might work. We have not treated many Eclectus parrots with homeopathy, but one responded well to pulsatilla. Acupuncture is used in these birds with fairly good results.

Macaws: It seems that about 50% of the macaws that pluck have significant internal disease, such as air sac abscesses, hepatitis, and chlamydiosis. A complete work-up is always indicated with these birds. Some remedies that might work with macaws include:

- tuberculinum avium
- sulphur
- phosphorus
- pulsatilla pratensis
- natrum muriaticum (especially in babies)

Case Examples of Birds that have Responded to Homeopathy for Feather Grooming Disorders

African Grey Parrot: There was an African Grey Parrot that had been abnormally grooming for eight months. The bird was a female and was chewing the feathers down to stubs, but there were no skin lesions. Blood tests, fecal exams and radiographs were all normal. The bird was shy and reserved, very uncomfortable with anyone other than the owner (timid, bashful). She would chew her feathers when the owner was present, but never when the owner paid close attention to the bird, and it was believed that this was an important aspect to consider.

She was very rigid about her thinking, and would not accept any new toys in her cage. The chewing behavior had started when the owner went away on a trip for three weeks (abandoned, forsaken feelings). It seemed like there was a significant amount of anxiety as well. Finally, the bird tended to pluck the most at twilight (generally aggravated at twilight).

The remedy pulsatilla pratensis was selected and she was given a 200C potency, with instructions to give it in the water once weekly for four weeks. About five years after the remedy was given the bird still had not chewed or plucked at all since the remedy, and she had become a much more outward, brave bird.

A Blue and Gold Macaw: This case is a Blue and Gold Macaw, male, that had been plucking for three years. The entire chest, abdomen and back were bald. The bird was wild caught as an adult (discontentment, longing, depression). He would commonly attack various members of the family when they least expected it, although he was a gentle bird most of the time. There seemed to be a lot of underlying anger as he would suddenly get into fits of squawking, attacking his toys and aggressively attacking his feathers. He would bang his beak on the perch repeatedly, as if in a rage. At other times he was calm and seemingly happy.

He was a very thin bird for his size, in spite of the fact that he had an excellent appetite (emaciation, despite eating heavily). He would masturbate with a toy several times daily (increased sexual desire). Several years prior, he had been extensively treated for a granulomatous air sac abscess.

The homeopathic remedy, tuberculinum avium, was used. First he was given a 30C dilution, once weekly for four weeks. When he was seen again, he had not stopped his plucking, but his caretaker believed that he was calmer. He was prescribed a 1M potency, once monthly for three months. At the three month exam, almost all of his feathers had grown in and he was much calmer. He had stopped biting the family members. We felt this to be a very good response, and decided to give no new remedies for the time being.

A year later, and he had returned to a somewhat lesser form of all of the above behaviors. We gave him another dose of 1M tuberculinum avium, which helped again, although not as much. He has continued to fluctuate back and forth between normal behavior and his old hyperactive, angry behavior, although he leaves most of his feathers alone now.

This is a good example of the effectiveness of homeopathy. But if the bird is left in the same environment that caused the problem to begin with (being wild caught, there will always be a longing to travel and be free), there is a tendency to return to the abnormal behavior.

Baryta Carbonica

Baryta Carbonica is best known as a remedy for the physically stunted, immature, runt of the clutch. If given to a young bird that is weaker, smaller and more timid than its clutch mates, it can restore strength and can improve the bird's growth and vital energy.

It is especially good for any bird that has delayed mental growth or maturity. Think of Baryta Carbonica when you have a bird that is not thriving and that food-begs all the time, refusing to grow up and start feeding on its own. Similarly, on the mental plane, it can bring maturity to an immature bird.

Belladonna

Belladonna is an excellent remedy for many acute emergencies: birds that are hot, show inflammation of the skin, are oversensitive to touch, sound or light, have marked swelling with heat and are in remarkable pain. Belladonna can help stop convulsions. It is effective for birds that are in an almost manic state, becoming suddenly angry and violent.

Belladonna is a good remedy for many infections anywhere in the body, especially the lungs, kidneys, ovaries and throat. Hot, swollen, painful sinus infections commonly respond to Belladonna. We have seen several hens start laying eggs again after taking Belladonna, even though they had reproductive tract disorders that fit the preceding description of symptoms.

Calcaria Carbonica

Calcaria Carbonica is a wonderful remedy to strengthen birds that are constitutionally weak. It is also great at preventing egg binding and soft-shelled eggs. During egg binding, give Calcaria Phosphoric; immediately after the egg has passed, change to Arnica.

Carbo Vegetabilis

Carbo Vegetabilis is known as the remedy that can revive a collapsed, dying patient. It can bring back the desire to live in the weakest, sickest bird. It restores the vital force in a most remarkable way. Give it to birds that are so weak they are almost comatose and to birds that are huddled in the corner, unable to rise. Use it with birds that feel cold to the touch.

It can also return strength to the psychologically exhausted, indifferent or apathetic bird. Some feather pluckers respond to this remedy when no other remedy will work.

Chamomilla

Chamomilla is one of our remedies for feather pluckers. (Actually, there are more than fifty remedies that might work.) It is also used for anger and irritability that have been suppressed for a long time. Macaws might fit this pattern, as do many Amazon Parrots. Chamomilla soothes and calms. It is often most effective at very low potencies to start with (perhaps a 6X). If it is successful, you can increase the potency dramatically over time.

Euphrasia

In old homeopathic writings, Euphrasia is commonly mentioned as a wonderful remedy for upper respiratory infections, especially when centered in or around the eyes. We have found this to be true when medicating chickens and ducks, but it is less helpful with parrot-type birds. If your bird's infection is more of a viral-caused problem, it will be more effective. Bacterial and chlamydial (psittacosis) problems respond better to different remedies (Mercurius, Phosphorus, Sulphur, Pyrogenium, Medorrhinum).

Hypericum

Hypericum comes from the plant St. John's Wort. It is often a wonderful remedy to calm birds, especially those that are of a nervous disposition and those that act like their nerves are on edge. More classically, we associate Hypericum with nerve damage and any type of injury or disease that adversely affects the nervous system. It might be helpful in low potency for some chronic immune diseases such as psittacine beak and feather disease.

Ignatia

Ignatia should be in every home alongside the Arnica. Ignatia is for all kinds of grief (also Natrum Muriaticum and phosphoric acid) both past and present. Birds are often like people; they develop grief for past events and never effectively deal with it. This "stuffed" emotion will then lead to physical or emotional problems.

Lachesis

A number of remedies are more targeted at fighting infections, and Lachesis is one of the best, especially when the infection is on the skin: open, weeping or oozing skin lesions that are hot and may be bleeding. There is often necrosis, or death of tissues, in the area of the problem.

   As with all remedies, there is also a mental effect to Lachesis. Birds that are extroverted and intense birds that start developing jealousy often respond to Lachesis. It is one of the remedies for feather-grooming abnormalities, biting birds and birds that seem to be hateful toward others in the home.

Lycopodium

Lycopodium is a wonderful remedy for birds. The classic mental picture of a bird that might benefit from Lycopodium is a bird that tries to maintain a confident outward appearance while being very afraid inside. These birds often try to bully other birds to get their way. If confronted by anyone, they suddenly turn fearful and withdrawn. Lycopodium can be very effective for many types of liver disorders, sinusitis, kidney problems, reproductive tract problems and intestinal disease, especially when the aforementioned mental picture is present. Lycopodium is a wonderful remedy for many Budgerigars (Parakeets) with tumors of the kidneys or gonads. It is one of the best remedies for a variety of behavioral disorders when these problems are generated by fear.

Nux Vomica

Nux Vomica is used for problems within the digestive system. The classic physical symptoms for which we would consider using Nux Vomica are vomiting, chronic diarrhea and crop binding. It is in the area of mental problems, however, that we find Nux Vomica most helpful. Birds with suppressed anger and the "type A" personality that becomes angry at everything may benefit. It therefore becomes an excellent remedy for some feather-grooming abnormalities. Because birds that are angry often suppress emotion and because suppressed anger often leads to congestion of the liver, Nux Vomica is one of the better remedies for birds with liver diseases.

Pulsatilla

Many birds are timid, mild and easily influenced and manipulated. They often need consolation when disturbed and get better when they have been consoled. These "wallflower" types will, over time, develop both physical and emotional problems. They may become fearful. They might be frantic to find their owners and become anxious when separated. Jealousy often follows. Behavioral problems include feather plucking, chewing under the wings until they bleed and becoming irritable with loved ones when the bird is at its most jealous.

Physically, birds with upper respiratory conditions, especially those that have a green to yellow discharge, might benefit from Pulsatilla. Chronic sinusitis with obstructed nostrils is a classic sign for Pulsatilla, especially when the bird's emotions fit this remedy. It can also be a wonderful remedy for many reproductive tract problems in hens including blood on the eggs, infertility and egg binding.

Rhus Toxicodendron

Rhus Toxicodendron is a great remedy for sore, painful joints and chronic arthritis. Many older birds will benefit from low-potency Rhus Toxicodendron on a daily or weekly basis. Birds with chronic wing injuries in which they hang their wings down might benefit. Stiff joints that get better after moving around a bit and in warmer weather are candidates for Rhus Toxicodendron.

Silica

Silica (Silicea) is one of the most commonly used remedies. On the mental plane, the bird that might need Silica is a bird that lacks internal strength, perseverance, determination or stamina. There is often a lack of self-esteem due to a general feeling of weakness. This often can lead to a paralysis of action in which the bird will often just sit around all the time, especially when stressed. Thus, Silica becomes another one of the remedies to consider for birds that pluck, chew or overgroom their feathers.

Birds that are chronically ill, delicate birds that can't withstand any stress, and birds that easily become weak and fatigued might benefit greatly from Silica. Silica is a cancer remedy and can be effective in cases of tuberculosis and other chronic infections. Poorly growing beaks and nails are signs that Silica should be considered. Chronic, dry nasal obstructions ("rhinitis") might heal with Silica.

Perhaps the single most "classic" use for Silica involves the treatment of abscesses. Silica will open and drain abscesses, bringing the infection to the surface. This may not necessarily be a good thing in a bird that has internal abscesses—in the lungs or liver, for example—because bringing the infection to the surface can spread it into other parts of the body. Silica should be used with caution in these cases.

In general, use Silica when you want to add strength to the physically frail or add true grit to the mentally timid, sensitive or yielding bird.

Sulphur

Sulphur (Sulfur) covers so many patterns of illness, it is hard to briefly describe its actions. It is simply the most commonly used remedy in homeopathy. Skin eruptions and self-traumatically caused wounds of the legs or wing webs, especially when these wounds are hot and red, might respond to Sulphur. It is an important remedy for liver disease, especially cirrhosis. Many cases of diarrhea, when the stool has a foul odor and is worse in the morning, will respond to Sulphur.

Birds that might respond to Sulphur include those that tend to be unkempt looking (possibly even a bit greasy looking), that have more body odor than most other birds and that tend to be a bit hot. Mentally, birds that might fit this remedy are often very outgoing yet have deeper anxieties because of their low self-esteem.

Sulphur is an excellent remedy for many birds with poor-quality feathers, bronzing feathers or greasy-looking feathers. It is high on the list of potential remedies for any bird that is plucking or chewing its feathers. It is excellent for many deep-seated illnesses including allergies, air sac disease, intestinal tract problems, papillomas and nose and sinus infections.

Symphytum

Symphytum is a remarkable remedy for bone healing. It rapidly speeds up the process and ensures that most fractures will heal. There is a caution with its use, however. It should never be given until the bone has been set; otherwise, it will start the healing process so rapidly that the bone will heal out of alignment.

With fractures, for the first twenty-four hours give Arnica and then follow with Symphytum for the next week. Follow that by giving Calcaria Phosphoric to finish the healing.

An Avian Homeopathic Repertory

BEAK

- **Cere, Brown Hypertrophy of**   arnica montana, graphites, lycopodium clavatum, pulsatilla pratensis
- **Cracked, easily**   antimonium crudum, natrum muriaticum, silicea
- **Dryness**   silicea, thuja occidentalis
- **Exfoliation**   arsenicum album, graphites
- **Overgrown, distorted**   calcarea carbonica, graphites, silicea, sulphur, thuja occidentalis

- **Liver disease, chronic**   argentum nitricum, carbo vegetabilis, chelidonium, calcarea carbonica, graphites, kali carbonicum, lycopodium clavatum, mercurius solubilis, natrum muriaticum, nux vomica, phosphorus, silicea, sulphur, thuja occidentalis

EXTREMITIES

- **Arthritis**

  - **Amazons, in**   ruta graveolens

  - **Budgerigars, in**   bryonia alba, kali iodatum, rhododendron chrysanthum, rhus toxicodendron, sulphur, *urtica urens*

  - **General**   aconitum nepellus, arnica montana, belladonna, bryonia alba, ferrum phosphoricum, kali iodatum, ledum palustre, lithium carbonicum, lycopidium clavatum, merdurius solubilis, natrum muriaticum, rhododendron chrysanthum, rhus toxicodendron, ruta graveolens, silicea, sulphur, tuberculinum avium

- **Broken bones**   symphytum

  - **Bruising, associated with**   arnica montana

- **Cold ameliorates**   kali sulphuricum, ledum palustre, pulsatilla pratensis, sulphur

Feet

- **Red and ulcerated**   sulphur

- **Paralysis**   argentum nitricum, cocculus indicus, gelsemium sempervirens, hypericum perfoliatum, kali carbonicum, plumbum metalicum,

- **Spraddle-legged**   calcarea carbonica, clacarea fluorica, calcarea phosphorica, fluoricum acidum, gelsemium sempervirens, phosphorus, silicea

EYES

- **Conjunctivitis**   euphrasia officinalis, pulsatilla pratensis, rhus toxicodendron

  - **Acrid**   euphrasia officinalis

  - **Purulent**   argentum nitricum, calcaria carbonica,chamomilla, euphrasia officinalis, hepar sulphuris, kali iodatum, lycopodium clavatum, *mercurius solubilis*, phosphorus, pulsatilla pratensis, sepia succus, sulphur, *zinc*

  - **Thick, pus**   euphrasia officinalis, *pulsatilla pratensis*, lycopodium clavatum

  - **Watery**   rhus toxicodendron

  - **Lacrimation**   graphites

  - **Photophobia, with**   graphites

FEATHERS

- **Beak and Feather Disease**   hypericum, sulphur
- **Bronzing, of**   arsenicum album, NUX VOMICA, *sulphur*
- **Growth, none**   arsenicum album, nux vomica, *selenium*
- **Grooming disorders (pluckers and chewers)**   arnica montana, arsenicum album, calcarea carbonica, folliculinum, ignatia amara, natrum muriaticum, *nux vomica*, phosphoricum acidum, sepia, silicea, sulphur, thallium, tuberculinum avium, veratrum album

  - **African Greys, in**   arsencum album, natrum muriaticum

  - **Separation anxiety, with**   natrum muriaticum

  - **Amazon parrots, in**   nux vomica, sepia, sulphur, veratrum album

  - **Females, in**   aconitum napellus, apis mellifica, calcaria carbonica, chamomilla, lycopodium clavatum, pulsatilla pratensis, silicea, sulphur

- **Males, in** apis mellifica, camphora officinarum, cantharis, conium maculatum, nux vomica, staphysagria, tuberculinum avium
- **Aggression, general** nux vomica, tuberculinum avium
  - **Cockatoos, in** arnica montana, arsenicum album, chamomilla, ignatia, natrum muriaticum, nux vomica, sepia,
  - **Males, in** nux vomica
  - **Females, in** pulsatilla pratensis, silicea
  - **Folliculitis, secondary to** hepar sulphuris, hypericum perforatum, kali bichromicum, mercurius solubilis, sarsaparilla, staphysagria, sulphur
  - **Frantic** belladonna, stramonium, veratrum album
  - **Macaws, in** nux vomica, tuberculinum avium
  - **Males, in** nux vomica
  - **Sexual** nux vomica, sepia

FEMALE

- **Binding, egg** calcarea carbonica, kali carbonicum, pulsatilla pratensis
  - **Blood on eggs, with** pulsatilla pratensis
  - **Soft-shelled eggs** calcarea carbonica, kali carbonica
- **Egg Laying** kali carbonica, lycopodium clavatum, pulsatilla pratensis, sepia,
  - **Soft-Shelled eggs** *kali carbonica*
  - **Stopping of** sepia
- **Infertility** natrum muriaticum, sepia, silicea
- **Ovarian cysts** arsenicum album, belladonna
- **Oviduct** kali carbonica, pulsatilla pratensis, sepia

GENERALITIES

- **Abscesses, Granulomatous** tuberculinum avium
- **Anemia** calcarea carbonicum, ferrum metalicum, plumbum metalicum, sulphur
- **Anesthesis, slow to recover** *acetic acid,* carbo vegetabilis, phosphoric acid
  - **Ailments from** acetic acid, carbo vegetabilis, hepar sulphurous, phosphorus, phosphoric acid
- **Cancer** calcarea carbonica, carcinosinum, graphites, *lycopodium clavatum*, nitricum acidum, phosphorus, silicea, sulphur, thuja occidentalis
  - **Budgies, in** calcarea carbonicum, carcinosinum, graphites, lycopodium clavatum
  - **Familial history of** *carcinosinum*, lycopodium clavatum
- **Candida albicans infections** calcarea carbonica, calcarea phosphorica, *china officinalis*, helonias dioica, lycopodium clavatum, medorrhinum, pulsatilla pratensis, natrum phosphoricum, nitricum acidum, sepia, thuja occidentalis
- **Emaciated** arsenicum album, calcaria carbonica, calcaria phosphorica, iodium, natrum muriaticum, nux vomica, lycopodium clavatum, pulsatilla pratensis, phosphorus, sepia, silicea, sulphur, tuberculinum bovinum
  - **Appetite, ravenous, with** baryta carbonica, baryta iodata, calcaria carbonica, calcaria phosphorica, causticum hahnemanni, china officinalis, cina, iodium, lycopodium clavatum, Natrum muriaticum, nux vomica, silicea, sulphur
- **Tobacco smoke, ailments from being around** gelsemium sempervirens, nux vomica, tabacum

- **Lead poisoning** alum, *aurum metallicum*, causticum, lycopodium clavatum, mercurius solubilis

- **Pyaemia** arsenicum album, calcaria carbonica, hippozaenium, *lachesis*, pyrogenium

- **Sepsis** arsenicum album, arsenicum iodatum, baptisia tinctoria, china oficinalis, crotalus horidus, echinacea angustifolia, *lachesis*

- **Trauma** aconitum napellus, arnica montana, hepar sulphuris calcareum, rhus toxocodendron, ruta graveolens, symphytum officinale

  - **Head, with seizures** belladonna

  - **Neurological symptoms, with** hypericum perforatum

- **Vaccinations, acute reactions** aconitum napellus, apis mellifica, belladonna, thuja occidentalis

  - **Ailments after** aconitum napellus, apis mellifica, belladonna, mercurius solubilis, hosphorus, silicea, suplhur, thuja occidentalis

- **Weakness, unable to rise due to severe illness** *carbo vegetabilis*

- **Zinc poisoning** aurum metalicum, mercurius solubilis

HEART

- **Cardiomyopathy** crataegus oxyacantha et monogyna, digitalis prupurea

- **Cyanosis** digitalis prupurea

- **Heart, general** crataegus oxyacantha et monogyna, digitalis prupurea, rhus toxocodendron

KIDNEY

- **General** arsenicum album, cantharus, kali carbonica, mercurius corrosivus, natrum muriaticum, phosphorus, pulsatilla pratensis

- **Gout** argentum nitricum, arnica montana, causticum hahnemanni, colchicum, bryonia alba, ledum palustre, *lycopodium clavatum*, rhododendron chrysanthum, rhus toxicodendron, *sulphur, urtica urens*

- **Paralysis** hypericum perforatum

  - **Renal tumors, with** arsenicum album, hypericum perforatum, *lycopodium clavatum*

- **Uric acid crystals increased, in droppings** argentum nitricum, arnica montana, urtica urens

LIVER

- **Liver Disease, general** NUX VOMICA, *lycopodium clavatum*, phosphorus

- **Fatty liver disease** calcaria carbonica, carbo vegetabilis, *chelidonium majus*, kali bichromica, kali carbonica, lyssinum (hydrophobinum), lycopodium clavatum, mercurius solubilis, *nux vomica, phosphorus*, picricum acidum, sulphur

MIND

- **Agitated, over-stimulated** lachesis, stramonium, veratrum album

  - **Outlet, without** ignatia amara, *lachesis*, nux vomica

- **Aggression** *nux vomica*, pulsatilla pratensis

- **Anger** arsenicum album, chamomilla, ignatia amara, lycopodium clavatum, nitricum acidum, *nux vomica*

  - **Underlying** nux vomica

  - **Violent** aconitum napellus, lycopodium clavatum, nitricum acidum, pulsatilla pratensis

- **Anxiety** ACONITUM NAPELLUS, argentum nitricum, arsenicum album, belladona, calcaria carbonica, calcaria phosphorica, cannabis indica, carboneum vegetabilis, conium maculatum, euphrasia officinalis, hyoscyamus niger, ignatia amara, kali carbonicum, kali nitricum, *lachesis, lycopodium clavatum*, mercurius solubilis, Natrum muriaticum, nitricum acidum, *phosphorus*, pulsatilla pratensis, sepia, silicia, sulphur, thuja occidentalis, veratrum album
- **Cowardness** gelsemium sempervirens, lycopodium clavatum
- **Dependant on others** baryta carbonica, pulsatilla pratensis
- **Fatigue, mental, from an inability to adapt to new surroundings** conium maculatum, *kali phosphoricum*, picricum acidum
- **Fear, violently throws self around cage** aconitum napellus, belladonna, lycopodium clavatum, nux vomica, *stramonium, veratrum album*
- **Grief** causticum hahnemanni, Natrum muriaticum
- **Irritability** kali sulphuricum, Natrum muriaticum, nitricum acidum, nux vomica, phosphorus, sepia
  - **Idle, while** calcarea carbonica
- **Jealous, bites owner when others approach** calcarea sulphuricum, hyoscyamus niger, lachesis, lycopodium clavatum, nux vomica, pulsatilla pratensis, stramonium
- **Rigid, unable to adapt to captivity** calcarea carbonicum, *kali carbonicum*
- **Sensitive** gelsemium sempervirens, natrum muriaticum, pulsatilla pratensis, silicia,
- **Timid** kali sulphuricum, pulsatilla pratensis

MOUTH

Pharynx

- **Inflamed, chronic** graphites, sulphur
- **Choanae elongated** phosphorus
- **Choanal papillae eroded** phosphorus

NERVES

- **Ataxia** arsenicum album, calcaria carbonica, nux vomica, phosphorus, plumbum metallicum, silicea, stramonium, zinc
- **Nerves, general** rhus toxicodendron, hypericum perforatum
- **Paralysis** argentum nitricum, cocculus indicus, gelsemium sempervirens, hypericum perforatum, kali carbonicum, lachesis, phosphorus, plumbum metallicum, zinc
  - **Renal tumors, with** hypericum perforatum, lycopodium clavatum
- **Seizures** aconitum napellus, belladonna, calcaria carbonica, ignatia amara, lycopodium clavatum, silicea
  - **Status epilepticus** aconitum napellus, belladonna
- **Weakness** iodium, nux vomica, plumbum metallicum, silicea, zinc, zinc phosphoricum

NOSE

- **Catarrh** graphites
  - **Colds, gets easily** graphites
- **Coryza** graphites
  - **Dry, obstructed** phosphorus

- **Pharyngitis**   nux vomica, phosphorus, sulphur
- **Sinusitis**   arsenicum album, bryonia alba, hepar sulphuris calcareum, kali bichromicum, kali nitricum, lycopodium clavatum, mercurius solubilis, Natrum muriaticum, nux vomica, phosphorus, pulsatilla pratensis, silicea

PEDIATRICS

- **Infantile behavior**   baryta carbonica
- **Separation anxiety**   nux vomica
- **Slow development**   calcaria carbonica
- **Stunted growth, in chicks**   baryta carbonica

RESPIRATORY

- **Chronic upper respiratory infections**   arsenicum album, graphites, sulphur

NUTRACEUTICAL AND HERBAL THERAPIES

We have often heard the statement that "we are what we eat." Although this statement may seem trite at times, it is actually understated. Nutrition is the foundation on which we build the long-term health of our birds. Simply stated, for our birds to be healthy physically, emotionally and mentally, we need to feed them the highest quality diet possible.

What is less understood is that nutrition and herbal medicine are not only powerful in maintaining health, they also are remarkably effective in treating diseases. According to the World Health Organization, herbal medicine is the single most popular form of medicine worldwide. Why? Because it is so effective. There is a very large amount of scientific data to back up this claim.

What do we do when our companions become ill? All too often, we move entirely into treating with allopathic therapies and traditional veterinary medicine. Serious illness may need Western medicine, but we know of no disorders that would not benefit from holistic therapies combined with allopathic medicine. Some diseases are best treated entirely with holistic therapies.

There are products available that are antibacterial, antifungal or antiviral. Others have been shown to boost the immune system or repair cells. There are antioxidants, detoxification factors and liver remedies. One drawback in utilizing these products is that there are so many different possibilities that it often becomes quite staggering. We will not attempt to cover this area of medicine in great detail, but we do include some of the better herbal and nutraceutical remedies that can be used for the benefit of our birds. Herbal medicine has long been the medicine of the people, and it should remain so. We recommend that you learn about it for both your benefit and your bird's.

Note that there are no scientifically proven doses for any of the products mentioned here. All doses provided are calculated based on a bird's size in relationship to the adult person's typical dose. Always start by dosing any herb at a lower dose than what is given, and slowly increasing the dose if no problems are seen. If doses are not provided, you must extrapolate down from the doses recommended for people that are given on the bottle. (A "typical" parrot might weigh 450 grams, or 1 pound; a "typical" person might weigh 130 pounds.)

In most situations, herbs and nutraceuticals should be used only for a couple of weeks at the most (unless directed otherwise by your holistic veterinarian).

ALOE VERA

You can use aloe vera squeezed from a freshly cut leaf of the plant itself, or you can use extracts placed into liquids or gels. Aloe is best known for its remarkable ability to heal burns, and it is just as effective at healing wounds. Use it topically for any cut, burn or scratch. It is very effective when given orally to boost immunity. It can also be given orally for its anti-inflammatory effects and its soothing quality on the intestinal system.

Dose: *1 drop orally for every 30 grams of body weight. It is safe topically if the bird licks it off.*

APPLE CIDER VINEGAR

Apple cider vinegar is a wonderful product for the health of the intestinal system. It has a number of beneficial vitamins and minerals. Perhaps it is most useful as an acidifier of the intestinal tract and the entire body. It can be placed into the water bowl daily when needed. Indications for its use include chronic disbiosis, candida infections, chronic gram negative bacterial infections, chronic diarrhea due to an abnormal bacteria in the intestinal system, foul-smelling stools and proventricular dilatation disease.

Dose: *1 to 2 tablespoons in 8 ounces of water. You can flavor it with a little honey. Use it at the only source of water for one to two weeks at a time.*

ASTRAGALUS

Astragalus is an excellent herb used extensively in Chinese Medicine and less commonly in Western herbal therapies. It is considered to be a powerful immune-system booster, especially when the digestive system needs immune boosting. Chinese medicine says it boosts the Qi of the body.

Astragalus can be used in birds as follows:

- For chronic diarrhea or chronic bacterial intestinal infections
- As a powerful immune booster, especially for problems in the intestinal system, pancreas and respiratory system

- To promote the healing of wounds

- To enhance energy and strength in debilitated birds

- To protect the body from bacterial and viral infections

- To help treat chronic lung disorders such as air sacculitis, bronchitis, shortness of breath and sinusitis

- To aid in the treatment of tuberculosis

- To strengthen kidneys and promote urine and uric acid excretion

- For bumblefoot

- To treat anemia of chronic disorders

Dose: *Chinese liquid extract, Astralgalus extractum, dosed at 1 to 2 drops for each 30 grams body weight. Use for two to four weeks.*

CHAMOMILE

Chamomile has pain-relieving, calming, anti-inflammatory properties. It is used quite often as a tea due to its soothing and sedative properties. It is effective for symptomatic relief of gastrointestinal disorders, but it should be used with other therapies to cure the patient. We like chamomile tea for birds that need calming such as feather pluckers.

Dose: *Boil and then use the tea in the bird's water bowl.*

CHAPARRAL

Chaparral is most widely known as an herb that treats cancer. It is very effective in this regard. It is often combined with red clover for cancer therapy. The primary ingredient that makes it a powerful antioxidant and anticancer herb is the compound nordihydroquaiaretic (NDGA). It also has analgesic, antiseptic and anti-arthritic properties.

CHROMIUM PICOLINATE

Chromium is an essential trace element. It is found in a cell's nucleus and helps strengthen the body's ribonucleic acid (RNA). It also strengthens the connective supporting tissues of the body. Since 1959, it has been known to be the active ingredient in the "glucose-tolerance factor" because it lowers blood glucose much as insulin does. It is excellent in helping to treat diabetics.

Brewer's yeast is relatively high in chromium and can be used with birds that often refuse to take chromium picolinate pills readily or accept them in food.

COENZYME Q10

Coenzyme Q10 is related to vitamin K. Coenzyme Q10 is used by the body to produce the energy it needs to live. Due to its energy-producing effect, Coenzyme Q10 can strongly boost the immune system in energy deficient individuals and people who have had chronic illnesses.

We would expect that Coenzyme Q10 would be beneficial for the following conditions:

- Heart disease
- Geriatric birds
- Diabetic birds
- Immune deficiency, especially the type that occurs with chronic illnesses
- Adjunct to cancer therapy
- Pharyngitis and sinusitis conditions

Dose: *1 milligram per kilogram of body weight one to two times daily.*

COLLOIDAL SILVER

Colloidal silver is reported to have antimicrobial effects. It has been used since before the 1900s for a large number of infections including viral, bacterial, protozoal and fungal.

Dose: *1 drop orally daily for most parrots (500-gram birds). Place 5 drops into a 4-ounce drinking bowl. Use it for one to two weeks.*

DANDELION

Dandelion is a potent diuretic; it increases the release of fluids out of the body through the kidneys. It can be very beneficial anytime there is a need to remove excess fluid from the body. It can be used for high blood pressure, congestive heart failure, yeast infections, diabetes, edema and kidney disease.

Dandelion increases the flow of bile through the liver and can be used in the treatment of liver disease when there is a need for increased bile production and excretion.

It is of particular benefit in treating liver disease when there is a buildup of biliverdin (yellow-stained urates in the droppings) and when associated with the buildup of excess fluid in the abdomen (ascites) that often develops with liver disease. It has little or no direct effect in healing liver cells or protecting them from damage.

Some veterinarians claim that dandelion and milk thistle should always be used together. This is not true because many of the disorders of the liver are not associated with bile retention and dandelion's diuretic effect will reduce blood flow through the liver, potentially harming it.

DIGESTIVE ENZYMES

The body's digestive system evolved with plant enzymes and expects to have them available to aid in digestion. Cooking at temperatures of even only 118°F will inactivate the natural plant enzymes found in food. The more we use cooked and commercial diets for birds, the fewer digestive enzymes we will see in our birds' diets.

Pancreatic enzymes (animal source digestive enzymes) are less effective in birds. They are inactive in an acidic environment such as in the crop and proventriculus of birds. Pancreatic enzymes must be used to pre-digest the food before feeding; plant enzymes do not have this problem.

Plant source digestive enzymes are often active in a wide range of pH conditions (pH 3.0 to 9.0), making them more effective throughout the digestive system.

Many birds benefit from the addition of plant source digestive enzymes. This includes:

- Birds with intestinal gas, voluminous stools or undigested food in the feces
- Crop-bound birds or birds with slow crop emptying
- Birds with allergies
- Chronically ill birds
- Birds with weight loss
- Birds with feather bronzing or muted colors to the feathers
- Birds with chronic intestinal bacterial infections
- Thin birds that seem to be weak and chronically ill

Dose: *20 milligrams per kilogram of bird weight, given with each feeding. Use for weeks or even longer.*

DIMETHYLGLYCINE

Dimethylglycine (DMG) is used to increase the amount of energy available to the body's cells. It can be used as an immune booster when chronic illness is present. It passes into the brain easily and can be used for some disorders of the brain including epilepsy or seizures.

Dose: *2 to 4 milligrams per kilogram of bird weight, offered every 12 to 24 hours.*

ECHINACEA

Echinacea is also called the purple coneflower and has been used as an immune booster in all animals, including birds, for a very long time. It is not one of the most potent immune stimulants, but it is very safe. It primarily boosts the part of the immune system used to fight viral infections, and it is most effective in the early stages of infections.

It has been widely reported that one should only use Echinacea for fourteen days at a time and then stop to rest the body, but there is no evidence to support this claim.

We might use Echinacea in the following situations:

- Early on in the course of any infectious condition

- For chronic rhinitis and sinusitis conditions

- At the onset of any viral infection within an aviary such as polyoma virus outbreaks

- For Candida (yeast) infections of the crop or intestinal system

- To aid in the treatment of psittacine beak and feather disease

ELDERBERRY

Elderberry, *Sambucus nigra*, has anti-inflammatory, alternative and antiviral activity. It has been shown to reduce flu symptoms for the average person by 40 percent. It is mostly being studied for therapy of colds and flu in people.

Elderberry can be made into a tea that can be given to birds in their water bowl. If you do this, you need to make sure the bird continues to drink; otherwise, dehydration could develop.

We would consider using Elderberry in birds for:

- Any viral infection

- Acute rhinitis and sinusitis

- Any skin disorder with a possible viral etiology

As a tea, it can be effective as an alternative for strengthening and balancing the body's functions when there is fever and dehydration.

Essiac

Essiac is an herbal preparation used in the treatment of cancer. It originated from Canadian Native Americans. The use of Essiac was revived in the 1920s by Rene M. Caisse. It contains Indian rhubarb (*Rheum palmatum*), Slippery elm (*Ulmus fulva*), Burdock root (*Arctium lappa*) and Sheepshead sorrel (*Rumex acetosa*).

Several herbal companies have modified the original recipe by adding other anti-cancer herbs such as red clover. Some of the separate ingredients have been shown to have antitumor effects and "blood cleansing" properties. It seems most effective in lessening the pain associated with cancer.

Feverfew

Feverfew, *Tanacetum parthenium*, lowers fevers and provides pain relief. In people, it is effective in helping relieve migraine headaches. It is a good herb for the treatment of nonspecific pain and inflammation, especially of the gastrointestinal system. It can be very effective, especially when combined with other herbs and vitamins in the treatment of chronic headaches.

Ginseng

Panax Ginseng is a potent immune and energy booster. It should not be used for more than a couple of weeks unless prescribed by your avian holistic veterinarian. Many times, it should be avoided in younger healthier birds.

Ginseng can be used for:

- Anemia

- Immune deficiencies

- Chronic diarrhea

- Chronic bacterial infections of the intestinal system

- Aiding cancer therapies

- Impotency

- Aiding recovery from debilitating illnesses

- Spermatorrhea (lack of sperm)

- Menorrhagia, cystic ovaries, infertile eggs

- Cachexia (severe weight loss)

- Promoting longevity in older birds

GLUCOSAMINE

Glucosamine sulfate is probably the best form of glucosamine to use. It is very effective in repairing joint damage and in alleviating the symptoms of arthritis.

We might recommend its use for:

- Inflammatory bowel disease

- Arthritis and degenerative joint disease

- Chronic colitis

- Food allergies

- Gout

- All geriatric birds

HAWTHORN BERRY

Hawthorn, *Crataegus laevigata*, is an excellent herb for support of the heart. It will lower blood pressure, regulate the beating of the heart and improve the heart's output. This is an excellent herb for many older birds that have marginal heart function. Birds with known heart murmurs might also benefit from its use.

MARSHMALLOW

Marshmallow, *Althaea officinalis*, has antitussive and expectorant properties, so it is good for coughs and bronchitis. It is an emollient, so it nurtures the skin. In general, it is good at cooling and moistening the body, especially in the areas of the lungs and bronchi, the stomach and the kidneys.

Although less is known about Marshmallow than about many other herbs, it is a very effective herb for a number of conditions including diabetes, chronic coughs, intestinal inflammation and ulcers. It also protects the liver from toxins and is effective for wasting diseases, skin diseases and any condition in which the body lacks moisture.

We might use it for birds with:

- Cloacal stones, uroliths

- Tuberculosis

- Conure bleeding syndrome

- Gastrointestinal inflammation, cloacal inflammation

- Feather-plucking disorders

MILK THISTLE

Milk thistle, *Sylibum marianum,* is a wonderful herb for the liver. It has been shown to protect the liver and heal liver cells. Its active ingredients are found in the fruiting bodies, the seeds and the entire plant. (The content of silymarin is highest in the fruiting body.) Although there are fewer liver-healing properties in the seeds, birds will readily eat these tasty millet-size seeds, making milk thistle seeds an excellent addition to the diet for any bird with liver problems.

There is a nutraceutical extract of milk thistle called silymarin, which is a flavonoid having an affinity for the liver. It is used quite commonly in Japan and Europe for acute liver toxicosis. It's primarily used to regenerate hepatocytes, where it improves the flow of bile and fat to and from the liver. If used in too high a dose, however, it can cause loose stools due to the increase in bile it produces.

Milk thistle, or silymarin, is one of the best herbs for liver cirrhosis, hepatitis, acute toxicosis of the liver and fatty liver disease. It is also beneficial for bile duct inflammation and is a potent anti-oxidant. Glutathione is one of the most important hepatic detoxification pathways of the body, and milk thistle increases glutathione content in the liver by up to 35 percent.

MULLEIN

Mullein, *Verbascum sp.,* is an herb that has emollient, antitussive, antispasmodic, pain-relieving, expectorant and wound-healing properties. It is often used for coughs, bronchitis, tracheitis, syringitis and other respiratory disorders.

It speeds wound healing and, when topically applied, is a pain reliever. This makes topical applications one of its better uses. We like to add it to aloe vera for wound healing and to garlic for inflamed areas with marked infection. It is also good for intestinal inflammation with diarrhea and bloody stools.

We would consider using mullein in birds for the following conditions:

- Self-traumatically induced lesions (chewing or scratching at the skin until it bleeds)

- Ear infections, especially when combined with garlic

- Coughs, voice loss, bronchitis, air sacculitis

- Diarrhea and droppings that have a lot of mucous, especially with bleeding

- Many gastrointestinal, respiratory, eye, skin and ear problems

PROANTHOCYANIDINS

Proanthocyanidins have many other names including Grape Seed Extract, Pine Bark Extract and Pycnogenol®. It is an excellent antioxidant and has actions somewhat similar to vitamin C. Beneficial effects of bioflavonoids include strengthening capillaries and regulating their permeability. Proanthocyanidins readily enter the brain, nurturing brain cells.

We might use proanthocyanidins for:

- Skin disorders

- Feather picking (only if there are pathological changes to the skin and follicle)

- Self-mutilation

- Bacterial folliculitis

- Brain disorders

- Damage to the blood vessels

- Poisonings

- Aging changes

- Retinal disease

- Heart disease

- Atherosclerosis in older Amazon Parrots

- Eclectus parrots with plucking or physical disorders (Eclectus Parrots seem to have an increased need for antioxidants. They often have chronic low-grade opportunistic bacterial overgrowth.)

RICE-BASED INTESTINAL SUPPORT PRODUCTS

UltraClear Sustain®, UltraClear Plus® and Ultra InflamX® are products that support the intestinal system, liver detoxification and intestinal inflammation, respectively. They are only sold through doctors, and they are wonderful products to help support a large variety of disorders in birds.

We might use these products for:

- Chronic diarrhea

- Food allergies

- Chronic vomiting in birds (especially when caused by gastrointestinal indigestion or malassimilation)

- Chronic Giardia-associated diarrhea

- Dysbiosis

- Hepatopathies/liver failure (use UltraClear Plus®)

- Detoxification strategies

- Allergic dermatitis

- Other immune-associated pathologies

- Chronic microbial gastrointestinal "infections" (Klebsiella, E. coli, Giardia)

- Dysbiosis and enterotoxemia

- Salmonella

- Chronic viral infections producing immune suppression (psittacine beak and feather disease)

- Gut microbial overgrowth following antibiotic use

ST. JOHN'S WORT

St. John's Wort, *Hypericum perofratum*, is currently one of the most popular herbs for people. It is said to be the herbal equivalent to Prozac®. It does have proven sedative and anti-depressant effects. It is also an anti-inflammatory and an astringent.

St. John's Wort can be applied topically to promote healing, or it can be taken internally. If taken for depression or anxiety, one needs to continue therapy for several weeks before any change might be expected.

As a homeopathic remedy, Hypericum has been used widely for a variety of nervous conditions, both mental and physical. St. John's Wort is said to be the Arnica of the nervous system and can be effective in traumatic conditions affecting the nerves. It can be used for neuralgia, anxiety and arthritic pains, either taken internally or applied topically.

We would consider using Hypericum for:

- Feather pluckers, when the condition seems painful or the bird seems depressed

- The treatment of certain chronic viral diseases (because hypericum has the ability to inhibit retrovirus in mice)

- Birds that tend to be irritable due to anxiety

Tea Tree Oil

Tea Tree Oil, *Melaleuca alternifolia*, is widely used as an antimicrobial therapy and may treat bacterial and fungal infections. It can be applied topically with a swab or directly from the dropper. It should never be taken internally because it is toxic. Even high external doses can cause tremors, depression and weakness. Tea Tree Oil has an oily nature and will spread onto the feathers, destroying their insulation abilities.

We do not recommend its use in birds.

Valerian Root

Valerian root, Valeriana officinalis, is an effective tranquilizer and sedative. It has no relationship to the Western pharmaceutical Valium®. It is widely used in Europe for nervous conditions, insomnia, convulsions, epilepsy and pain relief.

We might use Valerian for:
- Feather plucking
- Fearful birds, especially during thuderstorms, moving and traveling
- A bird that is being aggressive to its mate or caretaker

9
DISEASES AND POTENTIAL THERAPIES

When your bird seems to be ill, the first step is always to take it to a competent avian practitioner. The bird will need a Western medical diagnostic examination to determine the degree of illness. A holistic-minded veterinarian who is also an avian veterinarian is preferable, if there is one in your area.

It is important to know as accurately as possible how sick your bird is. We are not referring to a diagnosis of a specific disease; you must determine whether your bird is a little sick from the disease or very sick. Just running a fecal examination or a bacterial culture tells you nothing about how sick your bird is; only tests such as blood exams and radiographs (X-rays) are capable of determining the degree of illness. Birds that are very ill, meaning their vital systems are so out of balance that they could soon die from the illness, need hospitalization and emergency veterinary care. Western medicine is at its best when treating critically ill patients. It is much less successful when treating chronic diseases.

Birds that are not critically ill should always be medicated at home. Home care is far less stressful on the bird; only at home can the bird feel the love and caring that you, its caretaker and companion, can provide. Your careful attention will aid its recovery immensely. Request that your veterinarian teach you how to do the necessary treatments.

Regardless of the proposed Western medical therapies planned, holistic therapies can help your bird regain health. These therapies can be used either at the same time as

Western medicines or in place of traditional Western medical therapy, whichever is most appropriate. Even when your bird is critically ill, there are times when holistic therapies are the best course of action. This is when you need to consult a qualified holistic avian veterinarian. Because there are far fewer holistic veterinarians than are needed, many doctors provide telephone consultations for a fee. Most of these doctors require a local veterinarian to examine the bird before they make any recommendations for complementary or alternative therapies.

The following list of proposed therapies is intended to help guide you in your decision making. It is not intended to replace consultations with avian veterinarians and holistic veterinarians. Some of the therapies, such as acupuncture, should be administered only by a trained professional (an International Veterinary Acupuncture Society–certified, IVAS, veterinarian).

Some products mentioned here have not been covered in the text of this book. This is unavoidable; there is not enough space in this book to cover every possible therapy. We realize, however, that little information is available about holistic care for birds. The information is intended to guide both you and your bird's doctor. Some of the products mentioned are available only through a holistic veterinarian; others are commonly available through most herbal and nutritional supplement retail outlets. Many of these products are mentioned to give you some idea about what to do. Others are intended to give your holistic veterinarian some ideas for how to help, especially when the doctor is not particularly knowledgeable in bird medicine. It might be a good idea to take this book with you when you consult your veterinarian.

To acquire most of these products, we recommend that you contact a holistic veterinarian first. The "Resources" appendix lists associations of holistic veterinarians that can provide you with names of veterinarians in your area. Local holistic veterinarians will be familiar with sources of high-quality products. In addition, many of these products are widely available at health-food stores, vitamin stores and herbal shops. This appendix also lists sources of products; companies that sell homeopathics, herbs and nutraceuticals; and books that can provide you with more information about different aspects of holistic therapies.

Finally, if you see something you understand and can do, do it. Therapies you do not understand are potential areas for you to study while seeking holistic veterinary care.

Homeopathic remedies have various dilutions, C or X. When you purchase the remedies, you should be specific about what potency you want.

Therapies

Any Illness

Heat: This is most important for the smaller birds. Warm their environment to 85°F with about 60 percent humidity. For smaller cages, place a heating pad under the cage with a couple of layers of towels between the heating pad and the cage. Then wrap the cage with several layers of towels to hold the heat in. For larger cages, the room needs to be warmed up. You could also place a heat lamp on the bird. Avian veterinarians can also give you ideas for how to make hospital cages.

Sleep: If the cage is usually in a busy, noisy area where people are coming and going until late at night, the bird needs a new location in the home. Spare bathrooms often work great because the heat registers can be opened wide while the thermostat in the house is turned up only a little, causing the bathroom to heat up nicely.

Treat your bird at home: Some birds need hospitalization, but in our experience, most can be treated at home. Your bird will sleep better at home and will feel the love and security needed for rapid recovery. Most procedures employed at veterinary clinics can be taught to a willing caretaker including subcutaneous fluid therapy, injections of antibiotics, and feeding by hand or dropper.

All too often, a hospitalized bird might get subcutaneous fluid (something you can learn to do), a couple of shots each day, and lots of stress: dogs barking, lights glaring, late hours, veterinary technicians that may be afraid of your bird, and a generally chaotic experience. The bird might stop eating as a result, and the veterinarian will have to become more aggressive with forced feeding, which only increases the stress. The bird also might not be able to sleep, so its strength is sapped even further.

If you must hospitalize your bird: If you must hospitalize your bird, stop by and visit it. Some veterinarians will tell you that it's better for your bird not to see you while it is in the hospital. We have been hospitalizing and treating birds for twenty years and have never known that to be true. Do not accept a statement by your veterinarian that it is not possible to visit your bird frequently. Ask yourself what it would be like for you to be isolated in a hospital without any visits from your loved ones! Gently insist that you must see your bird and assure the doctor that you will stay out of the way. Most of the time when owners stop by, they can make sure the cage is being kept clean, can encourage their bird to eat, and can give it love. The bird's perkier attitude after a visit is heartwarming to see, and it often will go down to its feed cups and eat right after you leave.

Feed your bird its favorite foods: Don't worry about providing a balanced diet; a sick bird needs energy more than anything. Feed it what it will eat within reason. If the bird is hospitalized, bring its favorite foods to the hospital. A bird that is not eating will often take its favorite foods from its owner. Eat your meals with your bird—a sick bird will often eat if it sees you eating as well.

Beak and Nail Overgrowth

Beaks that grow long and need repeated trimming are a symptom of disease. The disease is often associated with the liver. (See the section later in this chapter that discusses liver treatments.) You can also improve the bird's diet. Higher protein, when associated with high-quality proteins, is important. Feeding egg yolks can be very helpful.

Many of these birds have weak thyroids as well as liver disease. (See the section later in this chapter about how to treat hypothyroidism.)

Use products containing herbs that help the body metabolize fats. This will remove them from the liver. These products are called lipotrophics. Seek holistic veterinary care to find out which lipotrophics are available.

Bleeding/Hemorrhage

If acute: Use ferric subsulfate (styptic or clotting powder) to cauterize; apply pressure with finger or bandage. Give Ferrum Phosphoricum 6C (homeopathic) twice daily.

If chronic: Find the cause and correct it. (See a veterinarian.)

Yunnan Paiyao is a Chinese herb that decreases bleeding. Mix powder into lactulose and give orally by dropper: two capsules in 15 ml, 0.5 ml daily for 500 grams body weight.

Causing shock: Give Carbo Vegetabilis 200C (homeopathic).

For fluid therapy, the veterinarian must do it or instruct you.

Trauma: Give Arnica 30C (homeopathic).

Bumblefoot/Sore Feet

Chinese herbal: Angelic and Mastic

Western herbs: Aloe vera juice, two drops per 100 grams body weight

Homeopathic: Ledum or Silicea, 6C

Acupuncture: SP 9, LI 11, Bafeng

Diet: Vegetables high in carotenoids (orange/yellow colored vegetables), vitamin E, vitamin C (fruits)

Topical: Aloe vera gel (can be mixed with antibiotics if needed)

Soak feet in disinfectant such as chlorhexidine or iodine. (Veterinarians can provide this.)

Broken, Bleeding Feathers

First, don't panic. We have never seen a bird bleed to death from a broken blood feather. Calmly evaluate and take action based on the following guidelines. You will need a towel in which to wrap your bird while restraining it to examine the affected feather.

Do not pluck out all bleeding blood feathers. Many will stop bleeding and will eventually grow in normally. If you remove the blood feather, a new one must then grow in after the one removed, and it also may break and bleed. Thus, it is often best to "nurse in" a blood feather instead of removing it.

If bleeding has stopped, do nothing and let the feather finish growing in normally.

If bleeding is mild or moderate, find the feather and apply pressure with your finger at the place the feather is bleeding until the bleeding stops (usually one to two minutes).

If bleeding is profuse, find the feather involved and pluck it out. Then pinch closed the follicle from which the feather came to stop the bleeding from the follicle.

If there's no bleeding now but the new feather is broken (severely damaged) or hangs sideways, find the feather involved and pluck it out. Then pinch closed the follicle from which the feather came to stop the bleeding from the follicle.

Burns/Cuts

Aloe vera: Squeezing the juice from the cut leaf of the plant itself is best. Almost all businesses that sell plants have aloe vera. Buy a plant and keep it on hand for emergencies for the whole family. Aloe vera gel or juice is also helpful.

Lanolin: Mix lanolin U.S.P. (any pharmacy can get this) with aloe vera gel.

Urtica urens or cantharis: 6C or 12X (homeopathics)

Diabetes

Diabetes is a serious illness that is not very effectively treated with insulin in birds. We have helped many birds using the following:

Chromium picolinate: This is excellent in promoting the utilization of insulin by the body. Cut the dose proportionally by the size of the bird as compared to the labeled adult dose. (This can be found at most pharmacies and herbal stores.) A small pinch of the powder can be placed on food once daily. A pill can be powdered and placed into an ounce dropper bottle with lactulose. Give 1 drop daily for each 100 grams body weight.

Alpha lipoic acid: This is also excellent in treating diabetes. Dose similar to chromium picolinate. This can be found in health-food stores or can be mail ordered.

Fiber: Higher fiber diets are very helpful. Use products containing psyllium as well as soluble fibers such as apple pectin (readily found in health-food stores, herbal shops or through your holistic veterinarian).

Crop Bound, Slow Crop

If your bird acts even a little sick, seek veterinary care. If your bird acts fine, add plant source digestive enzymes into the feeding formula. (Prozyme® is one commonly available product.) Thin the feeding formula to almost a watery consistency. Mix feeding formula 50/50 with UltraClear Sustain®. (A holistic veterinarian can supply this.)

Slippery elm bark: This is alcohol free. The Western herbal product can be obtained in herb stores or by mail order.

Probiotics: (beneficial bacteria, such as acidophilus, lactobacillus plus fructooligosaccharides—found in all health-food stores).

Diarrhea, Chronic

L-glutamine: This nutraceutical product is available at most health-food stores, by mail order or from holistic veterinarians.)

Probiotics: (beneficial bacteria, such as acidophilus, lactobacillus plus fructooligosaccharides—found in all health-food stores).

Apple cider vinegar: The unfiltered variety is available in health-food stores. Give 1 to 2 tablespoons in 8 ounces of water. You also can flavor it with a little honey. Use at the only source of water for one to two weeks at a time.

Digestive enzymes: Prozyme

Aloe vera: See the section on burns.

Rice-based intestinal support products: UltraClear Sustain® is available from holistic veterinarians.

Egg Binding

Egg binding may become a life-threatening emergency in a short period of time. Seek veterinary care immediately.

Acupuncture (by an IVAS-certified acupuncturist): This can both help the bird pass the egg and strengthen the bird to prevent future egg binding.

Calcium lactate: This is an excellent source of calcium. When powdered on foods, it can help prevent future problems. Do not put calcium syrups in the water; they can promote Candida growth and are not necessary. Calcium injections may help at times, but a veterinarian must give these shots.

If no veterinarian is available to see your bird and the bird is becoming very sick, you may be able to feel the egg in the abdomen and rupture it with your fingers. This can be a dangerous procedure for your bird because the eggshell might cut a hole in the oviduct, but this is rare. On the other hand, it is often a life-saving procedure for the critically ill bird. Once the egg is ruptured, the bird will feel much better. The egg will usually pass in a couple of days.

Juicing: Vegetables are very high in calcium and many other vitamins and minerals.

Exercise, exercise, exercise: Allow birds to be flighted or make them "fly" on your hand. Use jungle gyms.

Glandular therapy to promote a healthy uterus and ovary may prevent a recurrence. (Holistic veterinarians can provide this.)

Feather Grooming Abnormalities (Pluckers and Chewers)

Never apply a collar without veterinary supervision. Collars are very stressful, especially to a bird that is sicker than you thought. Only healthy birds should be collared by a veterinarian, and they should be closely supervised during application.

St. John's Wort, Valerian root, passion flower: These Western herbal products are available at health-food stores or by mail order. Low-alcohol extracts are best. Give one drop for each 100 grams of body weight twice daily.

5-Hydroxy L-Tryptophan: This nutraceutical product is available at health-food stores or by mail order. This product is very potent. You only need a few grains once daily given in food.

Bach Flowers: See Chapter 8 to determine which to use. These are available at health-food stores or by mail order.

Acupuncture (by an IVAS-certified acupuncturist): This is very helpful.

Chinese herbal formulas: Use only under the supervision of a trained holistic veterinarian.

Homeopathy: Combination formulas (those having several remedies in the same bottle) have had little success in our hands. Single remedies (classic homeopathy), when prescribed by a trained veterinary homeopath, can be very helpful.

Aloe vera (1 oz), water (1 pint), Rescue Remedy (5 drops): These can be used in a spray bottle to mist the bird several times daily. Change the water in the bottle every couple of days.

Western herbs such as Valerian, passion flower, and kava kava: These might be helpful. They are available at health-food stores or by mail order. Low-alcohol extracts are best. Powdered forms can be sprinkled lightly on food.

Give your bird plenty of toys that can be chewed: Clean cardboard boxes can be placed on top of their cages. (They love to chew them up and play nest box in them.) Soft wood, small limbs and twigs are also effective.

Gout

Glucosamine sulfate: This nutraceutical is available at health-food stores. It can be powdered lightly on food.

Kidney glandulars: These can be obtained from a holistic veterinarian.

Acupuncture: This is effective when done by an International Veterinary Acupuncture Society-certified veterinarian.

Boswellia: This Indian or Ayurvedic herb is available at health-food stores. It can be powdered lightly on food.

Turmeric: This Western herb is available at health-food stores or by mail order. It can be powdered lightly on food.

(Note: There are many good products for arthritis that contain several herbs and nutraceuticals together. See a holistic veterinarian for one of these products. Mail-order companies also carry them.)

Heart Disease

Hawthorn berry: This Western herb is available at health-food stores. It can be powdered lightly on food daily.

L-carnitine: This nutraceutical is available at health-food stores or by mail order. It can be powdered lightly on food daily.

Coenzyme Q10: This is widely available, even at most pharmacies. It can be powdered lightly on food twice daily.

Gingko biloba: This Western herb is available at health-food stores. It can be powdered lightly on food.

Heat Stroke/Hyperthermia

Rescue remedy: See the Bach Flower section.

If collapsed: Give Carbo Vegetabilis 200C (homeopathic).

Oral electrolyte drinks: Pedialyte® is available at grocery stores in the baby food section or at drug stores.

Natrum carbonicum, natrum nuriaticum: Give 30C. (Homeopathics should select one or the other.)

Put a few drops of water on the head and feet to cool the bird.

Get to a veterinarian as soon as possible.

Hypocalcemia (Low Blood Levels of Calcium)

This uncommon disease is often mistakenly diagnosed because of faulty lab test results. (Blood samples must be processed rapidly; otherwise, the calcium will always test as being too low, even when it actually was fine.)

The milk industry has brainwashed us into thinking that milk products are the best source of calcium. This is not true. There's essentially the same amount of calcium in one carrot as there is in a glass of milk. Juiced vegetables provide high levels of calcium.

Provide lots of vegetables in your bird's diet, especially dark green vegetables and carrots.

Calcium citrate is a well-absorbed supplement that can be placed on food. It is available at health-food stores and pharmacies and can be sprinkled on food daily.

Calcium deficiency is common in older women; all health-food stores are knowledgeable about good calcium supplements for women. These same products can be ground and fed to birds by adding a small pinch in their food daily.

Do not give your bird calcium supplements containing vitamin D unless it is specifically recommended by your holistic veterinarian.

Yogurt is nutritious and is accepted by most birds.

Hypothyroid (Low Thyroid Hormone Levels)

Hypothyroidism is one of the most overdiagnosed disorders in birds. Birds normally have very low thyroid levels that can easily be tested incorrectly by a lab as too low. A single blood sample for thyroid testing, which is what many veterinarians use, is completely useless. Our guess is that well over 90 percent of the birds diagnosed with this condition have been incorrectly diagnosed and should not be on replacement thyroid hormone therapy.

For a truly hypothyroid bird, you can use the following:

Glandulars (using the thyroid gland): These are processed to remove any active thyroid hormone. Holistic veterinarians can supply them, as can some mail-order companies.

Kelp: This and other iodine-rich foods such as seafood, yogurt and cheese can be effective.

Chinese herbal remedies: Consult a Chinese herbal medicine-trained holistic veterinarian.

In most cases, instead of using synthetic thyroid hormone, you should use organic thyroid hormone. (See your holistic veterinarian.)

Infections, Chronic/Immune Deficiencies

All birds experience most of the same bacteria and viruses. However, only a few birds, those with weakened and deficient immune systems, develop chronic infections. To be effective in treating these persistent problems, we need to boost the immune system as well as treat the infection. We like to use herbal antibiotics for these chronic problems.

Apple cider vinegar: The unfiltered variety is available at health-food stores. Give 1 to 2 tablespoons in 8 ounces of water. You also can flavor it with a little honey. Use this at the only source of water for one to two weeks at a time.

Candida or yeasts: Pau D'Arco, a Western herbal, is available at health-food stores or by mail order. You can powder it lightly on food twice daily.

Bacteria: Coptis is a Chinese herb available from your holistic veterinarian. Mail-order companies such as Nature's Sunshine all have products intended to be antibacterial therapies.

Viruses: You can use Chinese herbs or Western nutraceuticals. (Consult your holistic veterinarian.)

Liver Disease

Milk thistle

Dandelion (if droppings are stained yellow)

Glutathione

High-quality proteins, eggs

Licorice root

All of the preceding products are widely available at herbal shops, by mail order, and through your holistic veterinarian. Most companies that have a broad range of products will carry combinations of various herbs intended to treat the liver. Holistic veterinarians will also have these products. Some companies, such as Nature's Sunshine, have combination products as well.

Chinese herbal medicines are very effective in this instance. Consult an herbologist.

Oil, Grease on Feathers

Wash off the feathers using a gentle soap (such as Amway's LOC or any hand-washing dish soap) and warm water.

See the section about trauma later in this chapter.

Papillomas

Make a homeopathic nosode (a homeopathic remedy made from the diseased tissue) from a sample of the papilloma. (This can only be accomplished by a holistic avian veterinarian.)

Feed red pepper to the bird.

Aloe vera mixed with the Chinese herb Yunnan Paiyao can be applied topically (inserted into the cloaca through the vent) with a syringe (no needle) or pipette.

Sinusitis/Rhinitis, Chronic

You can employ nasal flushing or nose drops using saline, but do not give antibiotics. (You must be trained by a holistic avian veterinarian.)

Aloe vera: This can be used in a saline flush. (See your holistic avian veterinarian.)

Immune-boosting herbs: See the following section for these.

Acupuncture: SP 6, Yintang, LI4 (by an International Veterinary Acupuncture Society-certified veterinarian).

Chinese herbal formulas: Er Chen Wan or Gui Pi Wan can be prescribed by a veterinarian trained in Chinese herbal medicine.

Draining sinuses/antibacterial: Xanthium 12. (This ITM patent medicine can be prescribed by a veterinarian trained in Chinese herbal medicine.)

Oregon grape, mullein: These Western herbs are available at health-food stores and herbal shops or by mail order. You should use low-alcohol extracts. Give 1 drop per 100 grams body weight.

Soft-Shelled Eggs

Calcaria phosphoricum: Give 6C (homeopathic).

Juicing: Emphasize vegetables.

Parsley: Feed your bird fresh parsley daily.

Red clover: This Western herb is available at health-food stores and herbal shops or by mail order. You should use low-alcohol extracts. Give 1 drop per 100 grams body weight.

Organically bound calcium supplements: See the preceding hypocalcemia section.

Calcium citrate: Do not put calcium in water.

Surgery

Here are some things you can do to help your bird through anesthesia:

Slow recovery from: Phosphorus 200C (homeopathic). Request that your avian veterinarian give this if your bird is slow to recover from anesthesia or give it yourself in the recovery room.

Arnica 6C: This is for the bruising and trauma to tissues that always occurs with surgery. You can give it before and after surgery (homeopathic).

Bleeding after surgery: Phosphorus 200C (homeopathic).

Pain control: Aconitum 6C (homeopathic).

Feverfew: This Western herb is available at health-food stores and herbal shops or by mail order. You should use low-alcohol extracts. Give 1 drop per 100 grams body weight.

White willow bark: This Western herb is available at health-food stores and herbal shops or by mail order. You should use low-alcohol extracts. Give 1 drop per 100 grams body weight.

Rescue Remedy: See Bach Flowers.

Trauma

Rescue Remedy: See Bach Flowers Section (Chapter 8).

With bleeding: Yunnan Paiyao, a Chinese herbal combination, is excellent for reducing bleeding, but it only works when given internally. (It is not as effective with topical application.)

To stop bleeding (toes and skin): Apply ferric subsulfate. (If this is not available, try corn starch.)

Carbo vegetabilis: 30C (homeopathic). This is excellent to revive the comatose/listless patient.

Arnica: 30C (homeopathic). This is excellent for all types of trauma, whether physical or mental.

Heat: Warm birds by placing them in an 85°F environment.

Honey-water with a drop of dandelion to promote circulation can be given by dropper.

Zinc Toxicosis

Zinc toxicity is hard to determine because lab results are often inaccurate. If your bird is diagnosed with a zinc toxicity, the best way to treat it is as follows:

Remove the sources of zinc from the environment. Once the zinc is gone, the body rapidly rids itself of zinc. Your avian veterinarian can tell you where your bird might be getting exposed to zinc.

Don't use calcium EDTA (calcium versonate) unless the bird is critically sick. Calcium EDTA itself is highly toxic to the body.

Herbal chelation therapy also is effective. A number of herbal/nutraceutical supplements remove excess calcium and lead from the body, safely and effectively. Contact your holistic veterinarian.

Chapter 10
How to Choose a Holistic Avian Veterinarian or an Avian Veterinarian

Selecting an avian veterinarian for your bird is one of the most important things you'll do for your companion. Birds are so different from other animals that a specialist is necessary to maintain the optimum health of the bird. Not all veterinarians can meet a bird's needs. An avian veterinarian has studied birds as a specialty within veterinary medicine. A holistic avian veterinarian has added the study of alternative forms of medication to his or her knowledge bank and looks at the whole animal to keep it well or to return it to optimum health. An allopathic avian veterinarian tends to focus on the disease state that affects the animal.

The best time to choose an avian veterinarian is before you buy your bird. This gives you plenty of time to make a proper search as an informed consumer. Begin by asking questions of people at the pet store or breeder from whom you plan to buy your bird. Don't stop there, though. It's best to get several recommendations and to check each one as carefully as you would a physician for any other member of your family. Other good sources of information are local bird club members, knowledgeable friends who own birds and other veterinarians, many of whom will be glad to refer you to someone who specializes in birds.

After you've compiled a list of names, make appointments to interview the veterinarians. Ask questions of the veterinarian to be sure you can communicate and work together well. Expect to pay for this visit; the time you take up is time a paying client could have used. It is well worth your while to do this.

Have your questions ready. You may ask about methods of treatment, dietary recommendations for the species you plan to buy, caging requirements, the general personality of the species you plan to buy and its suitability for your personality and lifestyle. To what professional associations does this veterinarian belong? What kind of training has he or she had in handling birds? How many birds does this veterinarian include on his or her patient list? Does this veterinarian own birds? Does he or she talk about them in a way that indicates how important they are in his or her life? What kinds of emergency care are available? Is the person who answers the phone friendly and helpful?

Find out if the veterinarian is holistic or at least understands that holistic therapies have benefit. It is useless to try to establish a relationship with a veterinarian who is completely closed minded about the benefits of alternative and complementary therapies. After all, even the conservative American Veterinary Medical Association has recognized holistic medicine as a valuable adjunct to conventional Western medicine.

Appendix A

PREAMBLE TO THE AMERICAN VETERINARY MEDICAL ASSOCIATION

The preamble to the American Veterinary Medical Association (approved by the AVMA House of Delegates in 1996) reads as follows:

Veterinary medicine, like all professions, is undergoing changes with increasing rapidity. Additional modalities of diagnosis and therapy are emerging in veterinary and human medicine. [The AVMA guidelines for 1996] reflect the status of the role of these emerging modalities within the parameters of veterinary medicine for use in providing a comprehensive approach to the health care of non-human animals. Use of these modalities is considered to constitute the practice of veterinary medicine. . . . Such modalities should be offered in the context of a valid veterinarian/client/patient relationship. It is recommended that appropriate client consent be obtained. Educational programs are available for many of the modalities. It is incumbent upon veterinarians to pursue education in their proper use. It should be borne in mind that because the emergence and development of these modalities is a dynamic process, as time passes, the information may need to be modified.

Appendix B
A SPECIAL LETTER ON DYING PETS AND GRIEF

When a beloved companion becomes gravely ill, it is normal to be at your wit's end. This is a terrible time filled with sorrow, fear, possibly anger, hopelessness and uncertainty. Although these emotions grip us, we must make decisions for our pet.

What is the right decision? Is it to euthanize (humanely kill) our friend? When is the right time for this? What should we do with the body? Perhaps most importantly, what do we do now for our own well-being?

First you must understand that no one is more capable than you when it comes to making the necessary decisions. Whatever decisions you make, never, ever second-guess yourself. I have never seen anyone make the wrong decisions about their gravely ill companion when they make their decisions with the welfare of their friend in mind, when they make the decisions with love and compassion in their hearts.

Let's look at the issue of euthanasia. Should we euthanize our pet or let it die on its own? Should we take it home or leave it in the hospital? Our society seems to almost demand that we euthanize a sick animal "for the good of the animal." This may not be what you, or the animal, wants. Animals often appreciate being in the comfort of their home when they pass on. That often helps them die quietly and at peace. It is okay for you to make the decision to stop medicating them and to let them come home to be with you when they die. Again, only you can make the right decision.

Some birds want to fight to the end, and it is okay to make the decision to keep them alive as long as possible and never euthanize them. If you elect to keep your bird hospitalized, stop by and visit frequently. This will help both you and your bird a lot in the end. It will also help you with any decisions you might need to make.

Other birds need help to pass on and might wish to be euthanized. Look inside your own heart, and you will find the correct answer. It can be very humane to help them by choosing euthanasia for them.

If you decide to euthanize your bird, you must then decide whether to be with it at the end. Understand that your bird will be okay with whatever you decide. Some people need to be with their animal as it dies; it adds a degree of completeness that they are not able to achieve otherwise. Other people do not wish to be with their bird during the euthanasia, preferring to remember it in life, not death.

Either decision is fine as long as it fits with what you need. Again, ask yourself what you want and don't let the doctor, your spouse or anyone else influence you in any way.

Don't forget that some birds hide their illness so well that you might never know they are sick before you suddenly find them dead. Don't blame yourself for this. Rapid, unexpected death is part of life's experiences, and there is nothing you could have done to avert it.

Again, remember that you are the caretaker, the one who really knows what is best. Don't let any friend or veterinarian talk you into a decision that is not yours. You will make the right decision for your bird. Whatever feels right for you is probably right for your bird.

You also need to know that cremation services are available to dispose of your bird's body. For a slightly higher fee, you can have the ashes returned to you as well. You can then keep the ashes, bury them or scatter them at a place of your choosing. Another option is to bury your bird in your yard; if local laws do not allow for this, many areas have pet cemeteries.

Finally, know that your grief is normal. No, it wasn't just an animal. It was a kindred spirit, a friend, a companion and a loved one. Of course you will feel grief. You might feel such a great loss that you can't stand it. Please try to remember, however, that your companion's spirit will live on forever in your thoughts.

David McCluggage, DVM

Appendix C
RESOURCES

ONLINE RESOURCES

The following online resources provide names and addresses of both holistic avian veterinarians and avian veterinarians:

- Go to www.alvedmed.com to locate an alternative veterinarian in your area who specializes in birds. American Veterinary Medical Association, the Net Vet electronic 200, Parrot Preservation Society list of preferred veterinarians, Vet Quest and the Virtual Veterinary Center.

- At www2.upatsix.com/aav/search_aav.html you can find an avian veterinarian for your area, find out about the AAV and find other links to important bird sites.

- To learn about herbs: www.herbalgram.org

- To study bird conservation: www.fws.gov/

- To learn more about birds: www.enchantedlearning.com/subject/birds

All URLs were correct at the time of publication, but they are subject to change at any time. Use your Web browser to locate other lists by specifying "avian veterinarians" in your favorite search engine.

Books on Homeopathy

There are a number of different sources for books on homeopathy. A few sources are listed in other sections of this reference appendix. In addition to these sources, most suppliers of homeopathic remedies carry many of the books listed.

No single book can teach homeopathy. There are no short cuts to learning effective treatments. A number of books are available that list symptoms and then provide a few remedies for those symptoms. These books are far less effective than we would like. You simply must study from a good Materia Medica and repertory to be as effective as you can. The books listed here discuss theory of homeopathy and are quite helpful:

Boericke, William. *Materia Medica with Repertory,* 9th edition. Santa Rosa, California: Boericke & Tafel, Inc., 1927.

Bremness, Lesley. *The Complete Book of Herbs.* New York: Viking Studio Books, 1988.

Chapman, Beryl M. *Homeopathic Treatment for Birds.* Frome, Somerset, England: The C.W. Daniel Company LTD, Hillman Printers, 1991.

Hahnemann, Samuel. *Organon of Medicine.* [There are several publishers, and this is a very old book. It is the classic book that defined homeopathy, and it is a must read for the serious student. However, it is a very difficult book to read.]

Hering, C. *The Guiding Symptoms of Our Materia Medica,* a 10-volume edition. New Delhi, India: B. Jain Publishers, 1993.

Morrison, Roger. *Desktop Guide to Keynotes and Confirmatory Symptoms.* Albany, California: Hahnemann Clinic Publishing, 1993.

Sankaran, Rajan. *The Spirit of Homeopathy.* Bombay, India: Homeopathic Medical Publishers, 1991.

Vithoulkas, George. *The Science of Homeopathy.* New York: Grove Weidenfeld, 1980.

Suppliers for Homeopathic Remedies

B & T
281 Circadian Way
Santa Rosa, CA 95407

BHI
11600 Cochiti SE
Albuquerque, NM 87123

Boiron
6 Campus Boulevard, Building A
Newton Square, PA 19073
(610) 325-0918

Standard Homeopathic Co.
210 West 131st Street
Los Angeles, CA 90061

Washington Homeopathic Products
4914 Del Ray Avenue
Bethesda, MD 20814

BOOKS ON ORGANIC GARDENING

Lanza, Patricia. *Lasagna Gardening: A New Layering System for Bountiful Gardens: No Digging, No Tilling, No Weeding, No Kidding.* Emmaus, Pennsylvania: Rodale Press, 1998.

Yepsen, Roger. *1,000 Old Time Garden Tips.* Emmaus, Pennsylvania: Rodale Press, 1998.

HOW TO GROW YOUR OWN MEALWORMS

You first need to purchase a handful of worms from either a fishing-supply store or a company that sells these worms through mail order. Next, select a container such as a fish tank or a deep-sided, disposable pan commonly used to bake a turkey. Layer the bottom with burlap or another similar material and cover it with a few inches of wheat bran layering with burlap two or three times. Add the worms and feed them every week or two with chunks of raw apples and potatoes. Mist the top layer lightly every few days so the worms don't become dry. Keep the container in a cool, dark place. They will turn into shiny black beetles that will then lay eggs, which will hatch into mealworms that you can feed to your birds.

ABOUT THE AUTHORS

DAVID McCLUGGAGE, DVM

David McCluggage runs a holistic veterinary practice in Longmont, Colorado. He has practiced veterinary medicine since receiving his degree from Colorado State University in 1981 and has emphasized holistic care since 1991. His practice now includes a variety of different companion animals, primarily dogs, cats, birds and the occasional large animal.

Dr. McCluggage is a nationally recognized expert in avian medicine. He is a past president of the Association of Avian Veterinarians (AAV) and is a past chairman of the editorial committee of AAV. He was an alternate delegate to the American Veterinary Medical Association's House of Delegates. He is currently chairman of the Publications Committee of the American Holistic Veterinary Medical Association (AHVMA), is editor-in-chief of the Journal of the AHVMA and is a member of the Board of Directors of the AHVMA.

He has advanced training in homeopathy from the Academy of Veterinary Homeopathy, in acupuncture from the International Veterinary Acupuncture Society (IVAS) and in Chinese Herbal Medicine from IVAS. He is also an IVAS Certified Veterinary Acupuncturist. He is a past columnist for *Natural Pet Magazine*, is on the Board of Directors of the Natural Pet Products Association and has lectured widely in the United States, Canada and Europe on the topics of avian medicine and holistic avian medicine.

PAMELA LEIS HIGDON

Pamela Higdon is a freelance author and editor with a special interest in birds. After earning a Bachelor of Science degree in education from Texas Technological University, Pamela taught elementary school in Ras Tanura, Saudi Arabia. In that capacity, she developed and maintained a hands-on science room and an outdoor animal refuge for the elementary school. The refuge contained both wild birds and former pets. In addition, she kept birds both in her classroom and at home. Her focus was to educate young people and their families about the care of animals.

When she returned to the United States with her family in 1986, Pamela began to work for *Bird Talk* magazine as an editor and writer, furthering her interest and knowledge of birds. While at Fancy Publications, Pamela became the first managing editor of *Birds USA*, a yearly publication for those new to keeping birds. Since leaving Fancy Publications, Pamela has continued her interest in educating bird owners in the care of their pets by writing three books: *Lovebirds, Quaker Parrots* and *Bird Care and Training* for Howell Book House. She has also written articles for various publications, including *Bird Talk Magazine, Birds USA, Pet View* and *Natural Pet*. On a personal level, Pamela enjoys bird watching and caring for her birds at home.

Pamela became interested in holistic care for birds in the late 1980s. Her Vosmaeri Eclectus Parrots, Scarlett and Rhett, became ill with a klebsiella infection. Over the next two years, these formerly healthy birds contracted one bacterial illness after another, despite the use of antibiotics administered under the best of conditions. The birds recovered only after they were treated holistically.

Index